CHECK YOUR VOCABULARY FOR

MILITARY ENGLISH

A WORKBOOK FOR USERS

by

Richard Bowyer

Pe[illegible]ishing

First published in Great Britain 2001

Published by Peter Collin Publishing Ltd
32-34 Great Peter Street, London, SW1P 2DB

British Library Cataloguing in Publication Data
A catalogue record for this book is available from the British Library

ISBN: 1-901659-58-5

Text typeset by The Studio Publishing Services, Exeter EX4 8JN
Printed by Nuffield Press, Abingdon

Workbook Series

Check your:

Vocabulary for Banking and Finance	0-948549-96-3
Vocabulary for Business, 2nd edition	1-901659-27-5
Vocabulary for Colloquial English	0-948549-97-1
Vocabulary for Computing, 2nd edition	1-901659-28-3
Vocabulary for English: IELTS	1-901659-60-7
Vocabulary for English: FCE	1-901659-11-9
Vocabulary for English: TOEFL	1-901659-68-2
Vocabulary for Hotels, Tourism, Catering	0-948549-75-0
Vocabulary for Law, 2nd edition	1-901659-21-6
Vocabulary for Marketing	1-901659-48-8
Vocabulary for Medicine, 2nd edition	1-901659-47-X
Vocabulary for Military Terms	1-901659-58-5

Specialist English Dictionaries

English Dictionary for Students	1-901659-06-2
Dictionary of Accounting	0-948549-27-0
Dictionary of Agriculture, 2nd edition	0-948549-78-5
Dictionary of American Business	0-948549-11-4
Dictionary of Automobile Engineering	0-948549-66-1
Dictionary of Banking & Finance, 2nd edition	1-901659-30-5
Dictionary of Business, 3rd edition	1-901659-50-X
Dictionary of Computing, 4th edition	1-901659-46-1
Dictionary of Ecology & Environment, 4th edition	1-901659-61-5
Dictionary of Government & Politics, 2nd edition	0-948549-89-0
Dictionary of Hotels, Tourism, Catering	0-948549-40-8
Dictionary of Human Resources, 2nd edition	0-948549-79-3
Dictionary of Information Technology, 3rd edition	1-901659-55-0
Dictionary of Law, 3rd edition	1-901659-43-7
Dictionary of Library & Information Management	0-948549-68-8
Dictionary of Marketing, 2nd edition	0-948549-73-4
Dictionary of Medicine, 3rd edition	1-901659-45-3
Dictionary of Military Terms	1-901659-24-0
Dictionary of Printing & Publishing, 2nd edition	0-948549-99-8

For details about our range of English and bilingual dictionaries and workbooks, please contact:

Peter Collin Publishing
32-34 Great Peter Street, London, SW1P 2DB
tel: +44 20 7222 1155   fax: +44 20 7222 1551
email: info@petercollin.com   website: **www.petercollin.com**

Introduction

The worksheets in this workbook contain a variety of exercises appropriate for students requiring a working knowledge of English military terminology. The worksheets can be used either for self-study or in the classroom and can be completed in any order. Several have 'extensions': short classroom exercises based on the language in the main exercise. All the questions within this workbook are based on the *Dictionary of Military Terms* (published by **Peter Collin Publishing**, ISBN 1-901659-24-0).

This workbook is aimed at students with at least an intermediate level of English. However, many people involved in the military have to use English on a regular basis so students with a more basic level of English may therefore already have the passive vocabulary to handle many of the exercises.

Specialist vocabulary

It is important to appreciate that 'knowing' specialist vocabulary involves more than simply recognising it.

- You can understand the meaning of a word when reading or listening and yet be unable to remember that same word when speaking or writing.

- You may remember the word, but use it incorrectly. This can be a grammatical problem, like knowing that 'import' can be used both as a noun and as a verb. Or it may be a question of collocation: we use mail-order, not post-order.

- Then there is the question of the sound of the word. Can you pronounce it? And do you recognise it when you hear it pronounced?

For these reasons - memory, use and sound - it is important that students practise specialist vocabulary so that they can learn to use it more confidently and effectively. The exercises in this workbook will help students to expand their knowledge and use of marketing vocabulary.

Photocopiable material

All the worksheets can be legally photocopied to use in class. If, as a teacher, you intend to use most of the book with a class you may find it more convenient for the students to buy a copy each. You are not allowed to photocopy or reproduce the front or back cover.

Using the Dictionary of Military Terms

All of the vocabulary taught or practised in this workbook is in the *Dictionary of Military Terms*. The Dictionary gives definitions in simple English which students can read and understand. Many of the examples and definitions in the workbook are taken directly from the dictionary. Students should have a copy of the *Dictionary of Military Terms* to refer to when completing the exercises; using the dictionary is an essential part of successful language learning.

Structure of a dictionary entry

Each entry within the dictionary includes key elements that help a student understand the definition of the term and how to use it in context. Each term has a clear example, and part of speech. This is followed by example sentences and quotations from newspapers and magazines that show how the term is used in real life. These elements of the dictionary are used to create the questions within this workbook.

Vocabulary Record Sheet

At the back of the book is a *Vocabulary Record Sheet* (p54). Recording useful vocabulary in a methodical way plays a key role in language learning and could be done, for example, at the end of each lesson. The dictionary is a useful tool for ensuring that the personal vocabulary record is accurate and is a good source for example sentences to show how words are used, as well as for notes about meaning and pronunciation, etc.

Contents

Contents

Using the workbook

Most students find it easier to assimilate new vocabulary if the words are learned in related groups, rather than in isolation. For example, words frequently occur in the same context as their opposites and, as such, it makes sense to learn the pairs of opposites together (*see worksheets on page* 24.) Similarly, mind maps encourage students to look for connections between words (*see worksheet on page* 7). The exercises and activities in this workbook have all been grouped into sections. These sections practise different elements of military vocabulary, enabling the student to gain a fuller understanding of the words learnt.

The first section, **Word-building** (*pages* 1-7), encourages the student to identify links between words and to learn words that are morphologically related (for example, verbs and nouns which have the same stems). Within the **Parts of Speech** (*pages* 8-17) section, the emphasis is on understanding meanings and how to use terms in their correct grammatical forms. The worksheets in the third section practise the **Pronunciation** of military vocabulary (*pages* 18-21). The section **Vocabulary in Context** (*pages* 22-41) includes topic-specific exercises such as those on 'Radio conversations' and 'Offensive and defensive operations'. The activities in the last section, **Puzzles & Quizzes** (*pages* 42-54), expand students' knowledge and use of vocabulary in a fun way.

Communicative crosswords

Included in the last section are three communicative crosswords. These are speaking exercises where students complete a half-finished crossword by exchanging clues with a partner. There are two versions of the crossword: A & B. The words which are missing from A are in B, and vice versa. No clues are provided: the students' task is to invent them. This is an excellent exercise for developing linguistic resourcefulness; in having to define words themselves, students practise both their military vocabulary and the important skill of paraphrasing something when they do not know the word for it.

Using communicative crosswords

Stage 1 - Set-up. Divide the class into two groups - A and B - with up to four students in each group. Give out the crossword: sheet A to group A, sheet B to group B together with a copy of the ***Dictionary of Military Terms.*** Go through the rules with them. Some answers may consist of more than one word.

Stage 2 - Preparation. The students discuss the words in their groups, exchanging information about the words they know and checking words they do not know in the ***Dictionary of Military Terms***. Circulate, helping with any problems. This is an important stage: some of the vocabulary in the crosswords is quite difficult.

Stage 3 - Activity. Put the students in pairs - one from group A and one from group B. The students help each other to complete the crosswords by giving each other clues.

Make sure students are aware that the idea is to help each other complete the crossword, rather than to produce obscure and difficult clues.

- What's one across?
- *It's fired when attacking the opposition.*
- A type of gun?
- *No, it's what is loaded into a gun.*
- Ammunition?
- *Yes, that's right.*

A A	B B
A A	B B

Students work in groups, checking vocabulary

Alternatively, students can work in small groups, each group consisting of two As and two Bs and using the following strategies:

i) defining the word
ii) describing what the item looks like
iii) stating what the item is used for
iv) describing the person's role
v) stating what the opposite of the word is
vi) giving examples
vii) leaving a gap in a sentence for the word
viii) stating what the word sounds like.

A B	A B
A B	A B

Students work in pairs, co-operating to solve their crosswords

Word association 1:missing links

Each of the sets of four words below can be linked by another word. All the words are related to military matters. What are the missing words? Write them in the centre of the charts. The first one has been done for you as an example.

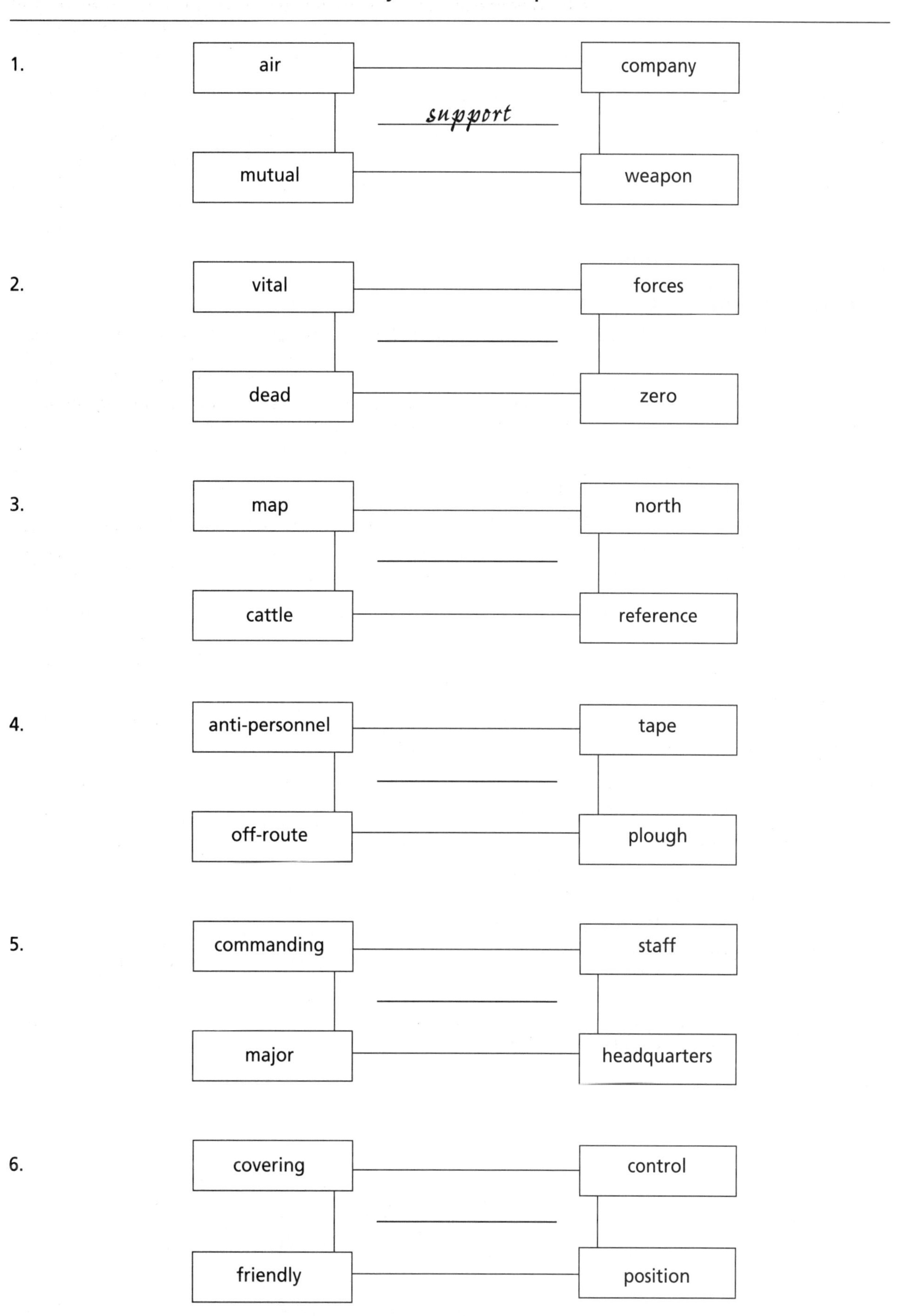

Two-word expressions

Make 14 two-word expressions connected with military matters by combining words from the two boxes: A and B. Then match each expression with the appropriate phrase. Use each word once. The first one has been done for you as an example.

Box A.

compassionate • voice • exclusion • supply • harrassing • ~~home~~ • shock
manoeuvre • field • pincer • distress • observation • static • flight

Box B.

zone • gun • ~~defence~~ • signal • leave • post • action • dump
path • procedure • line • fire • warfare • movement

1. Defence of a State's own territory in the event of war.

   home defence

2. Area or region, which the armed forces or shipping of another State are not allowed to enter.

   ____

3. Holiday granted to a service man who has problems at home.

   ____

4. Standard words and expressions which are used when talking on the radio.

   ____

5. Sign or message signifying that a person, ship or aircraft is in danger.

   ____

6. Covert position from which an area of ground may be watched.

   ____

7. Temporary store of ammunition, food, fuel, etc., in the field.

   ____

8. Method used to open a parachute as the parachutist jumps out the aircraft.

   ____

9. Tactical manouevre, in which two groupings attack an enemy force at the same time, but from different directions.

   ____

10. Random bombardment of a likely enemy location, in order to disrupt his activities.

    ____

11. Course taken by an aircraft or missile.

    ____

12. Military doctrine which recommends the use of mobility and constant aggression.

    ____

13. Artillery piece designed to be moved easily over all types of ground.

    ____

14. Sudden or aggressive attack or counter-attack, especially by tanks.

    ____

Word formation: nouns

A fast way to expand your vocabulary is to make sure that you know the different forms of the words you learn. Rewrite the sentences below, changing the verbs (which are in *bold)* to nouns. Do not change the meaning of the sentences, but be prepared to use some different words if necessary. The first one has been done for you as an example.

1. The enemy have ***advanced*** as far as Reichenbach.

   The enemy advance has reached Reichenbach

2. We should expect to ***lose*** at least ten percent of our aircraft.

3. The enemy started to ***withdraw*** at last light.

4. I will arrange for the vehicle to be ***recovered.***

5. They ***attacked*** under cover of smoke.

6. You must ***register*** all the targets by 1600 hours.

7. We will ***land*** the troops at night.

8. The reinforcements were delayed when the bridge was ***destroyed.***

9. It took seven hours to ***fly*** to Cyprus.

10. We were not informed that they were ***retreating.***

11. They are still ***clearing*** the route.

12. 6 Platoon will ***reconnoitre*** the enemy position.

Word marriages: nouns

Some nouns are formed by joining two words together to form a single word. Fill the gaps in the sentences below by combining a word from column A with a word from column B. The first one has been done for you as an example.

Column A
cease
search
~~life~~
foot
counter
way
road
guard
mine
fog
war
break

Column B
bridge
through
room
horn
~~boat~~
measure
head
light
point
fire
field
block

1. He was drowned when the ___lifeboat___ capsized.

2. There has been an enemy ______________ to the north of Brno.

3. A series of explosions informed us that a patrol had walked into the ______________ .

4. The ______________ will come into effect at 1100 hours tomorrow.

5. The missile had been fitted with a nuclear ______________ .

6. Our next ______________ is the track junction at grid 491370.

7. The tank used its ______________ to illuminate the target.

8. The ammunition will be kept in the ______________ for the night.

9. We found a small ______________ three hundred metres downstream.

10. We couldn't see the ship, but we heard its ______________ .

11. We have set up a ______________ on every route into the town.

12. As a ______________ against ambush, all convoys will be escorted by troops.

Word association 2: partnerships

Fill the gaps in the sentences below by linking an adjective from the column on the left with a noun from the column on the right. The first one has been done for you as an example.

Adjectives
chemical
high-velocity
~~first~~
air
collateral
negligent
interior
multinational
classified
corrugated
thermal
stealth

Nouns
information
bomber
discharge
damage
agent
image
iron
bullet
photograph
lines
force
~~aid~~

1. All the men are being given training in *first aid* .

2. These shells contain some sort of ______________________________ .

3. A ______________________________ is being deployed to the area.

4. The airstrike caused some ______________________________ to the adjoining residential area.

5. This night-viewing device produces a high quality ______________________________ .

6. He was court-martialled for passing ______________________________ to the media.

7. A ______________________________ has been shot down over enemy territory.

8. He was killed when one of his comrades had a ______________________________ inside the APC.

9. He was hit in the chest by a ______________________________ .

10. We can use our ______________________________ to redeploy the division.

11. You must revet the trenches with ______________________________ .

12. The Ops Officer has asked for an ______________________________ of the area.

Three-word expressions

Make 10 three-word expressions connected with military matters by combining words from the three lists: A, B and C. Then match each expression with the appropriate phrase. Use each word once. The first one has been done for you as an example.

A	B	C
foreign	protective	missile
immediate	aircraft	position
~~forward~~	target	device
general	piloted	disorder
final	object	drill
post-traumatic	action	authorized
remotely	~~air~~	force
laser	ballistic	damage
improvised	deployment	designator
primary	task	vehicle
joint	stress	fire
inter-continental	explosive	~~controller~~

1. Air-force officer or NCO who is attached to ground troops to direct close air support.

   forward air controller

2. Standard procedure to be carried out in the event of something going wrong.

   ____

3. Missile which flies from one continent to another and then ends its flight by simply falling onto the target.

   ____

4. Home-made bomb.

   ____

5. Pre-selected position that a unit or sub-unit will occupy in the event of war.

   ____

6. Mental collapse as a result of a horrific experience.

   ____

7. Small unmanned radio-controlled aircraft designed to carry surveillance equipment.

   ____

8. Pre-determined artillery target, registered on or just in front of your own position.

   ____

9. Device which projects a laser beam onto a target in order to illuminate it for a laser-guided bomb or missile.

   ____

10. Number of aircraft allocated to a unit for the performance of its operational role.

    ____

11. Large combined arms grouping involving different branches of the armed forces, which is formed for a specific operation or campaign.

    ____

12. Damage to an aircraft, caused by a loose object being sucked into its air intakes.

    ____

Word association 3:mind maps

A mind map is a way of organizing vocabulary to show the connections between words. This mind map is based on the word 'headquarters'.

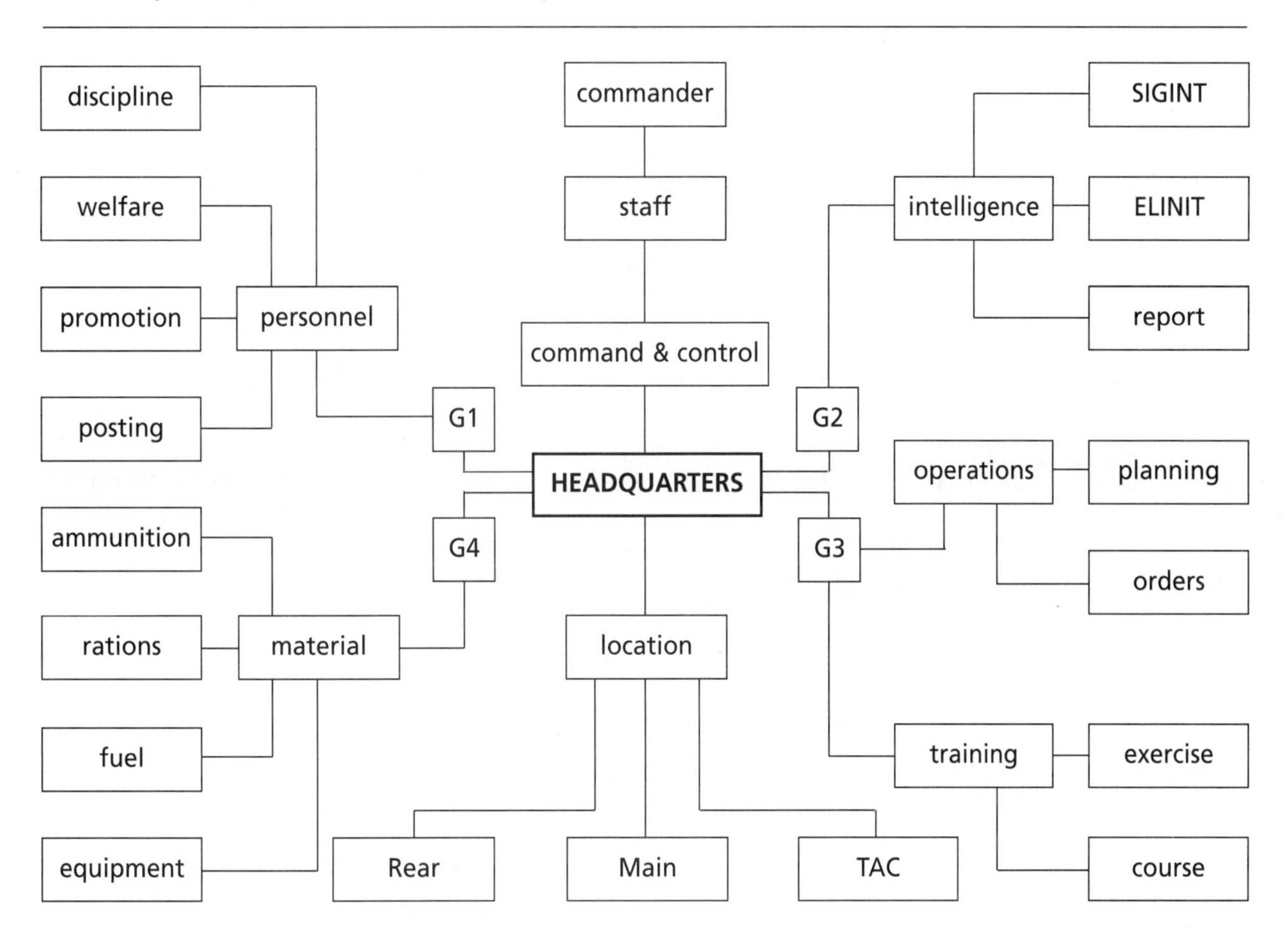

Exercise 1. Find words in the mind map to fit the following definitions.

1. Department which is responsible for the resupply of ammunition. ____________
2. Small mobile headquarters used by the commander on the battlefield. ____________
3. Act of raising a service man to a higher rank. ____________
4. Group of officers and other ranks who assist the commander. ____________
5. People who are employed by an organization. ____________
6. Information about the enemy. ____________
7. Moving troops and equipment as part of a planned military task. ____________
8. Detailed instructions given by a commander to his subordinates. ____________
9. Information obtained by listening to the enemy's radio transmissions. ____________
10. Act of practising the skills which units have to carry out on operations. ____________

Exercise 2. Design a mind map for one or more of the following:

- the army or navy or air force
- operations or logistics
- casualty

Nouns 1

All the nouns in the box relate to military matters. Use them to complete the sentences below. The first one has been done for you as an example.

fireplan	northing	~~password~~	resistance	frontage
flagship	intsum	demolition	pillbox	O Group
wreckage	trace	riot	interdiction	fallout

1. The sentry shot him because he didn't give the correct ___password___ .
2. This squadron's primary role is the ______________ of the enemy's supply routes.
3. The approach to the bridge is guarded by a ______________ .
4. Your limit of exploitation is the five - seven ______________.
5. The CO's ______________ is at 1400 hours.
6. The whole area has been contaminated by ______________ .
7. The battle group's position has a ______________ of five kilometres.
8. All our routes and report lines are marked on the ______________ .
9. Tell the battery commander to send us a copy of the ______________ .
10. We found ______________ of the aircraft scattered across the hillside.
11. The Admiral's______________ was hit by an Exocet missile.
12. The enemy losses were included in the last ______________ .
13. The bridge has been prepared for ______________ .
14. It started as a peaceful demonstration, but it quickly turned into a ______________ .
15. The forward units are encountering stiff______________ from the enemy rearguard.

Nouns 2

All the verbs in the box relate to natural and man-made features in the landscape. Use your dictionary to find the meanings of any which you do not know.

field • church • re-entrant • wood • quarry • road • railway line
mountain • factory • hedge • T-junction • village • bridge • summit
river • forest • copse • hill • spur • town • castle • crossroads
orchard • track • pass • saddle • knoll • ridge • lake • farm

Now look at the picture below, and match the nouns to the numbers.

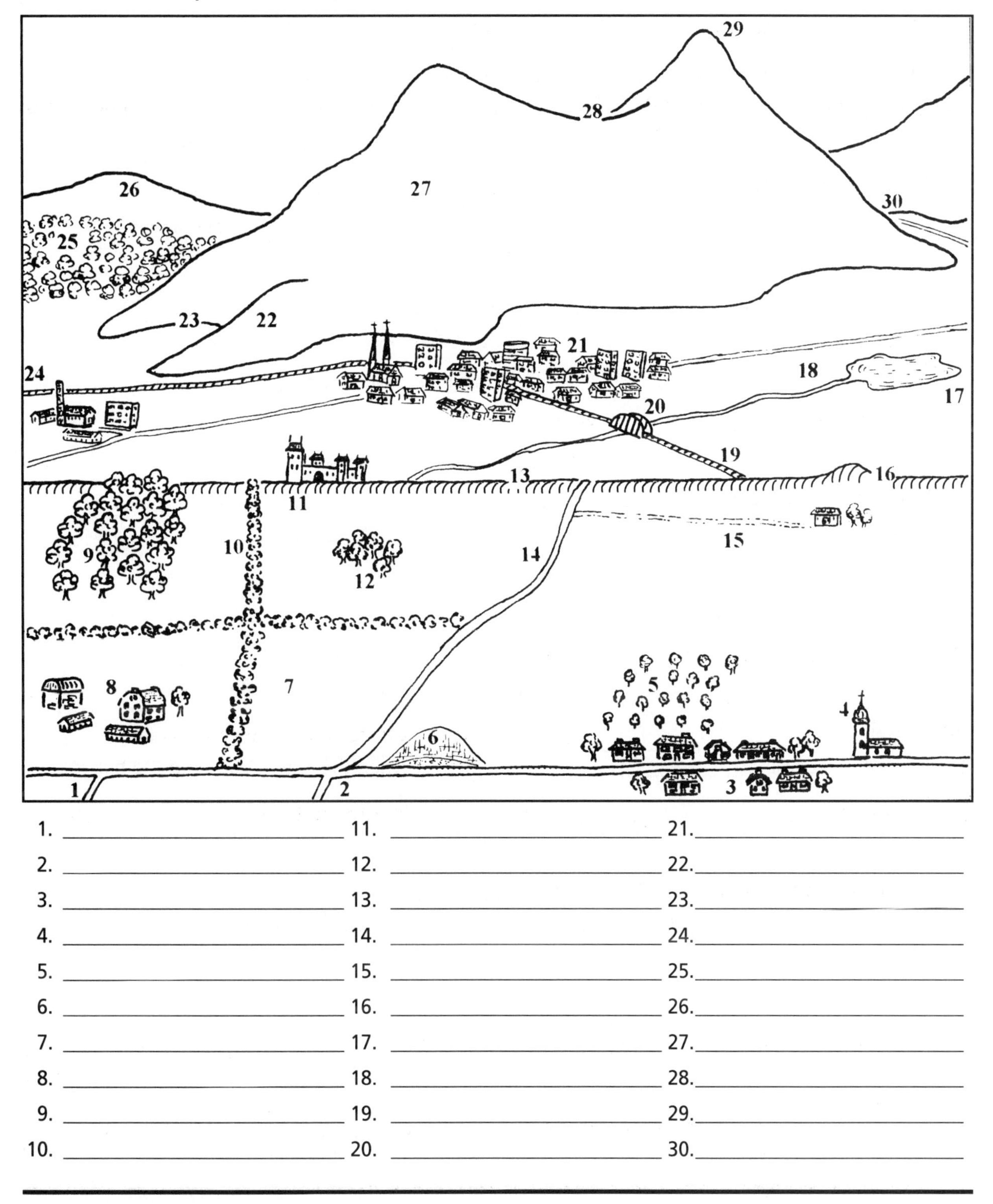

1. ______	11. ______	21. ______
2. ______	12. ______	22. ______
3. ______	13. ______	23. ______
4. ______	14. ______	24. ______
5. ______	15. ______	25. ______
6. ______	16. ______	26. ______
7. ______	17. ______	27. ______
8. ______	18. ______	28. ______
9. ______	19. ______	29. ______
10. ______	20. ______	30. ______

Adjectives

All the adjectives in the box relate to military matters. Use them to complete the sentences below. Each adjective should be used once only.The first one has been done for you as an example.

non-persistent • wire-guided • diversionary • untenable • self-propelled
incendiary • ~~secure~~ • subordinate • hostile • optical • civilian
unserviceable • preparatory • multirole • combat-effective

1. All units are equipped with ___*secure*___ radios.
2. Our battalion carried out a ______________ attack on the left.
3. The enemy shelled the position with a ______________ blood agent.
4. Any movement in that area should be considered ______________ .
5. The tank's ______________ instruments were damaged by shrapnel.
6. There is a ______________ gun in the farmyard.
7. The village was destroyed by ______________ bombs.
8. Less than sixty percent of our units are still ______________ .
9. All ______________ commanders are to attend the briefing.
10. Our position became ______________ when the enemy captured the hill.
11. This aircraft is a ______________fighter.
12. The attack was preceded by a ______________ bombardment.
13. The radio was ______________ after he dropped it in the river.
14. The enemy have been bombing ______________ targets.
15. The tank was destroyed by a ______________ missile.

Verbs: present continuous

The present continuous tense is used to describe an action which is happening at the moment. First, look at the verbs below, and use your dictionary to find the meanings of any which you do not understand.

retreat • advance • counter-attack • form up
~~brief~~ • withdraw • reorganize • assault • debus

Now look at the pictures below. They illustrate the sequence of an attack. Complete each sentence, using one of these verbs in the present continuous tense. The first one has been done for you as an example.

1. He *is briefing* ______

2. They ______

3. They ______

4. They ______

5. They ______

6. The enemy ______

7. They ______

8. The enemy ______

9. The enemy ______

Verbs: present perfect

The present perfect tense is often used to show how a past action can have an effect on what is happening now. The present effect is usually so obvious that it is not necessary to mention it. Look at the two columns below and match the present effect to the past action. The first question has been done for you as an example.

Past Action	Present Effect
1. The commanding officer has been killed. •	• a. The area is contaminated.
2. We have captured a brigadier. •	• b. We cannot talk to them.
3. Our tank has lost a track. •	• c. He is dead.
4. Heavy fog has grounded our fighters. •	• d. It is at sea.
5. B Company have withdrawn. •	• e. It is no longer an obstacle.
6. The enemy have captured a copy of the plan. •	• f. It is disabled.
7. There has been a chemical . attack at Bingen •	• g. He is a prisoner.
8. All the bridges have been blown. •	• h. They are cut off.
9. We have exhausted our ammunition. •	• i. I do not know what the plan is.
10. We have lost communications with C Company. •	• j. They are no longer holding their position.
11. The Guards have crossed their line of departure. •	• k. They cannot take off.
12. The enemy have surrounded D Squadron. •	• l. We cannot cross the river..
13. Our engineers have breached the minefield. •	• m. The operation is compromised.
14. The fleet has left the harbour. •	• n. We cannot fire our weapons.
15. I have not read the orders yet. •	• o. They are advancing.

Verbs: mixed tenses

All the verbs in the box relate to military matters. Use them to complete the sentences below. You may have to change the forms of the verbs to fit the grammar of the sentences. (Remember the five forms of English verbs - for example: *take; takes; took; taken; taking.*) The first question has been done for you as an example.

arm	relieve	~~interrogate~~	intercept	suppress
replenish	commandeer	jam	bridge	insert
deploy	shell	strafe	camouflage	mask

1. The prisoners were ___*interrogated*___ by an officer from the Intelligence Corps.

2. We have ______________ an enemy radio transmission.

3. Enemy fighters ______________ the refugee column, in order to clear the road.

4. The patrol will ______________ by helicopter at 1930 hours.

5. We managed to ______________ a civilian bus.

6. His weapon ______________ because it was rusty.

7. The position was ______________ by small-arms fire.

8. The battle group is ______________ into attack formation.

9. They are ______________ the vehicles with hessian and pieces of foliage.

10. The enemy have ______________ the river between Mistelbach and Bocksdorf.

11. That line of hills will ______________ our line of retreat.

12. Rations and water will be ______________ at 2130 hours.

13. You ______________ the rocket by pulling out this pin.

14. The enemy has been ______________ C Company's position for over an hour.

15. I will ______________ you in two hours.

Verbs: active/passive

Without changing the meaning, rewrite each sentence using a verb from the box in the passive form. Remember that it is not always necessary to mention the subject of the active sentence. The first one has been done for you as an example.

conceal • assassinate • breach • sink • shel • blow • ~~shoot down~~
ambush • intercept • compromise • capture • outrange

1. We destroyed three enemy fighters during the battle.
   Passive: *Three enemy fighters were shot down during the battle.*

2. Last night, someone shot the Chief of Police.
   Passive: ______

3. They hid the weapons in an old oil drum.
   Passive: ______

4. An enemy submarine has torpedoed HMS Brilliant.
   Passive: ______

5. The engineers have demolished the bridge at Zemun.
   Passive: ______

6. The enemy have taken the airfield.
   Passive: ______

7. Enemy artillery is firing at B Company.
   Passive: ______

8. Partisans opened fire on the convoy as it was moving through the gorge.
   Passive: ______

9. We have cleared a lane through the minefield.
   Passive: ______

10. The enemy is listening to our radio transmissions.
    Passive: ______

11. The enemy tanks can shoot further than ours.
    Passive: ______

12. Some local people have seen our OP.
    Passive: ______

Phrasal verbs 1

Phrasal verbs are quite common in military English. They consist of two words: a verb and a preposition. Match each phrasal verb below with its correct definition. The first one has been done for you as an example.

Phrasal Verb	Definition
1. pick up	a. to resupply a fighting vehicle or aircraft with ammunition
2. dig in	b. to abandon a position or location in a hurry
3. stand to	c. to be ready to do something.
4. mop up	d. to collect people or things with an aircraft, boat or vehicle, in order to transport them to another location
5. take off	e. to move forwards as fast as possible
6. bomb up	f. to be awake and at battle stations, in order to receive an enemy attack
7. push on	g. to admit that you cannot do something
8. roll up	h. to be guided towards something
9. stand by	i. to dig trenches or prepare other field fortifications
10. give up	j. to leave the ground
11. fall in	k. to clear an area of any enemy who remain after their main force has withdrawn or been defeated
12. bug out	l. to assault through an enemy position sideways, destroying or capturing it trench by trench
13. home in	m. to rest or wait in a concealed position before continuing a patrol or other covert operation
14. lie up	n. to continue to defend or resist
15. hold out	o. to take your place on a formal parade

Phrasal verbs 2

Use the phrasal verbs from the previous page to complete the sentences below. You may have to change the forms of the verbs to fit the grammar of the sentence. The first one has been done for you as an example.

1. The squadron ______took off______ while the airfield was being shelled.
2. We ____________________ in a small wood and observed the road.
3. B Company are ____________________ around the bridge.
4. If the enemy capture that hill, they will be able to ____________________ the entire position.
5. The installation was destroyed when a missile ____________________ on its radar system.
6. We had to ____________________ when C Company's position was overrun.
7. After several abortive assaults, the enemy ____________________ and withdrew.
8. The patrol was ____________________ by submarine.
9. The men collected their weapons and ____________________ outside company headquarters.
10. We ____________________ until last light. Then we were forced to withdraw.
11. Sunray says that we must ____________________ and capture the position.
12. D Squadron are still ____________________ their vehicles.
13. The company ____________________ for most of the night, after one of the trip-flares went off.
14. Two platoons are ____________________ to provide back-up.
15. The battalion has been ____________________ isolated groups of guerrillas in the hills.

Don't forget to keep a record of the words and expressions that you have learnt, review your notes from time to time and try to use new vocabulary items whenever possible.

Prepositions

The sentences in this exercise contain mistakes. The mistakes are all in the prepositions and there are three types:

1. missing preposition:	**I spoke ^ him about this last week**	*to*
2. wrong preposition:	**We're meeting again ~~in~~ ^ Tuesday**	*on*
3. no preposition:	**I'll telephone ~~to~~ you tomorrow**	

Find the mistakes and correct them.

---

1. He is currently based at Germany.
2. Load by sabot!
3. We debussed in front the enemy position.
4. They only have enough rounds to one more fire mission.
5. A Company captured of their objective thirty minutes ago.
6. The second command is Major Bunbury.
7. H-Hour is on 0545 hours.
8. We were unable recover the damaged vehicle.
9. We moved to the exercise area with bus.
10. He was charged of cowardice.
11. The enemy attacked to B Company's position last night.
12. We came in fire as we were crossing the town square.
13. We've just received a message by Brigade Headquarters.
14. USS Nimitz is already on sea.
15. Captain MacDonald is at leave.

Don't forget to keep a record of the words and expressions that you have learnt, review your notes from time to time and try to use new vocabulary items whenever possible.

Word stress

One of the keys to English pronounciation is *stress* - one syllable is emphasized more than the others. There are three possible pronounciations for three-syllable words:

A: Stress on the first syllable ❶ ② ③ **For example: *che* - mi - cal**

B: Stress on the second syllable ① ❷ ③ **For example: log - *ist* - ics**

C: Stress on the third syllable ① ② ❸ **For example: ref - u - *gee***

First look at the sentences below and find all the three syllable-words. Underline them and then classify them by putting them in the correct columns in the table on the right. There are twenty-four words in total. The first one has been done for you as an example.

1. The whole area is out of bounds to troops.
2. That information is classified.
3. The company commander has been wounded.
4. We must intercept the convoy before it crosses the river.
5. He was posted overseas.
6. The saboteurs were shot as they tried to escape.
7. We have established an OP on that hill.
8. We still don't know the enemy's intentions.
9. The engineers are preparing to demolish the bridge.
10. Our position is untenable.
11. My signaller was unable to repair the radio.
12. We will try to resupply you tonight.
13. We are going on exercise next week.
14. There has been an accident on the range.
15. The division will start to disembark at first light.
16. The brigadier had to countermand the order.

Group A ❶ ② ③
area

Group B ① ❷ ③

Group C ① ② ❸

Present simple

Verbs in the present tense add an 's' in the third person singular: I shoot, you shoot, he shoots. There are three different ways of pronouncing the 's'. Look at these examples:

A: /s/, for example *protects* B: /z/, for example *moves* C: /iz/, for example *releases*

Find the third person singular present tense verbs in these sentences and classify them by their pronounciation. Put them in the correct columns in the table on the right. Be careful: some sentences have more than one verb. There are 25 examples in total. The first one has been done for you.

---

1. The red light warns the operator when the device detects a chemical agent.
2. He commands a squadron of tanks.
3. Although he discharges his routine duties well, he always panics under fire.
4. In this demonstration, the squad skirmishes onto the objective and then reorganizes.
5. This vehicle clears obstructions and, if necessary, destroys them with its gun.
6. Sarin attacks the central nervous system.
7. This lever controls the missile as it flies towards the target.
8. Cpl Jenkins issues leave passes and travel warrants.
9. The aircraft usually drops GP bombs in support of ground forces.
10. The missile arms itself as it launches.
11. My platoon practises NBC drills at least once a month.
12. This vehicle tows a field gun and also carries its ammunition.
13. The Queen's Guard marches down this street every morning.
14. This chemical disperses after only five minutes.
15. The company digs trenches whenever it halts.
16. This missile scatters bomblets over its target area.
17. This watch-tower covers all three roads into the harbour.

Group A: /s/

Group B: /z/
warns

Group C: /iz/

Extension. The same rule applies to plurals: /s/ bullets; /z/ rounds; /iz/ cartridges. Look at the sentences again, and find four plurals in each pronounciation category.

Past simple / past participle

Regular verbs have three different pronounciations in the past tense (or the past participle). The difference is in the sound which you use for the ending. Look at these examples:

A: /t/, for example *attacked* **B: /d/, for example *ordered*** **C: /id/, for example *retreated***

Find the past forms of all the *regular* verbs in these sentences and classify them by their pronounciation. Put them in the correct columns in the table on the right. Be careful: some sentences have more than one verb. There are 25 examples in total. The first one has been done for you.

1. We assaulted the enemy position on foot.
2. He was based in Germany for five years.
3. The battle group advanced towards its objectives.
4. The shell exploded in the middle of the company RV.
5. He was killed when the lorry crashed.
6. The enemy mined the entrance to the harbour.
7. A local shepherd guided us over the mountain.
8. The crowd dispersed when we used CS gas.
9. The enemy launched a Scud two minutes ago
10. We engaged the tank, but missed it with both of our rockets.
11. They were resupplied with ammunition and fuel.
12. Last night, they bombed the Brigade Administration Area.
13. H-Hour has been delayed.
14. We reorganized in a wadi and then moved back.
15. They towed the vehicle into the wood and dumped it in a clearing.
16. At H+13, the mortars checked firing.
17. We covered A Company as they withdrew.
18. I sited the SF on our right flank.
19. He aimed at the leading vehicle.
20. They captured the bridge last night.

Group A: /t/

Group B: /d/

Group C: /id/
assaulted

Timings

The twenty-four hour clock is always used in military timings and to avoid confusion, the word 'hours' is normally added to the end. This is usually written as 'hrs'.

For example: ***The briefing is at 1430 hrs.***

Now write the timings below ***as you would actually say them.*** **The first one has been done for you as an example.**

1. 1625 hrs sixteen twenty-five hours
2. 0400 hrs ______________________
3. 1545 hrs ______________________
4. 0910 hrs ______________________
5. 2009 hrs ______________________
6. 1059 hrs ______________________
7. 1330 hrs ______________________
8. 1800 hrs ______________________
9. 0043 hrs ______________________
10. 2000 hrs ______________________
11. 0306 hrs ______________________
12. 2110 hrs ______________________
13. 2218 hrs ______________________
14. 1717 hrs ______________________
15. 0005 hrs ______________________

Extension: Work with a partner to practise saying timings. One person writes a timing as numbers (for example: ***1625 hrs*****) and the other then says it (for example:** ***sixteen twenty-five hours*****)**

Odd one out

In each set of words, one is the *odd one out*: different from the others. Find the word that is different and circle it. For example:

captain	**sergeant**	**lieutenant**	**major**

'sergeant' is the odd one out. All the others are officers.

1. frigate	destroyer	submarine	corvette
2. machine-gun	mortar	howitzer	field gun
3. guerilla	mercenary	soldier	partisan
4. minelayer	minesweeper	mine plough	flail
5. rations	fuel	reinforcements	ammunition
6. tank	APC	self-propelled gun	lorry
7. hill	bridge	embankment	church
8. Phantom	Apache	Tornado	Harrier
9. midshipman	admiral	sub-lieutenant	colonel
10. HE	HEAT	HESH	APDS
11. Sarin	hydrogen cyanide	anthrax	mustard
12. B-1	B-2	F-117A	F-22
13. Forger	Foxbat	Fantan	Fishbed
14. engineers	cavalry	artillery	infantry
15. pistol	assault weapon	light machine-gun	cannon

Don't forget to keep a record of the words and expressions that you have learnt, review your notes from time to time and try to use new vocabulary items whenever possible.

Multiple meanings

Some words have more than one meaning. For example an *operation* is a planned military task ('*this will be a covert* operation') but it is also an act of surgery ('*he needed an* operation *to remove the bullet*'). Can you identify the following eight words? Two or more meanings are given for each word.

1. This word means:
   - a rapid and aggressive movement towards the enemy. ***He was killed leading a bayonet ______________________ .***
   - an official accusation of a crime or offence. ***You are on a ______________________ for insubordination.***
   - an explosive device. ***One ______________________ failed to detonate.***
   - electrical energy. ***None of these batteries have any ______________________ left.***

2. This word means:
   - a tactical formation where men or vehicles move side by side. ***The squad advanced in ______________________ .***
   - electrical cable used to connect field telephones. ***"We must lay more ______________________ back to HQ".***
   - a length of rope. ***He threw a ______________________ to the men in the lifeboat.***

3. This word means:
   - a moving ridge of water. ***A huge ______________________ broke over the bows of the ship.***
   - one of several groupings attacking one behind the other. ***The first ______________________ was decimated.***

4. This word means:
   - to complete an exam or test successfully. ***You must ______________________ the Battle Fitness Test.***
   - a document allowing someone to do something. ***Show me your leave ______________________ please.***
   - a narrow route through the mountains. ***The ______________________ was blocked with snow.***
   - an aircraft's approach flight towards its target. ***We hit the plane on its second ______________________ .***

5. This word means:
   - a natural or man-made place where ships can shelter. ***The entrance to the ______________________ was mined.***
   - a secure area in the field where troops can rest. ***We set up a ______________________ in the wood.***

6. This word means:
   - a sign made by gestures, light or any other means. ***The ______________________ to withdraw is a red flare.***
   - a radio message. ***We've just received a ______________________ from Brigade HQ.***
   - electromagnetic waves transmitted by a radio. ***I'm getting a very weak ______________________ .***

7. This word means:
   - to block the enemy's radio transmissions. ***The enemy is trying to ______________________ us.***
   - to stop firing because of mechanical failure. ***Your weapon will ______________________ if you don't clean it.***

8. This word means:
   - detailed instructions for an operation. ***The OC is giving his ______________________ in thirty minutes.***
   - formal parade where disciplinary matters are dealt with. ***You will be on CO's ________________ today.***
   - document showing the day's programme and other information. ***Have you read squadron. ______________________ ?***

Opposites

Group 1 consists of adjectives which relate to military matters. Group 2 consists of nouns which are frequently associated with those adjectives.

First look at the adjectives in Group 1, and identify pairs of opposite meaning. Write these pairs in column A. Then write the nouns from Group 2 in column B, matching each one with its associated pair of adjectives.

One line has been done for you as an example.

GROUP 1

~~enemy~~ • passive • frontal • covert • strategic • magnetic
~~friendly~~ • tactical • mobile • active • blank • air-portable
overt • live • acting • mechanized • forward • static
rear • substantive • wheeled • flanking • tracked • grid

GROUP 2

bombing • rank • vehicle • ~~forces~~ • defence • ammunition • bearing
operation • night-viewing device • infantry • attack • area

Column A	Column B
enemy friendly	*forces*

Extension: Work with a partner to test one another. One person closes the book while the other asks questions. For example: *"What's the opposite of enemy?"*

What do I do?

When you work with other units and formations, you may well have to deal with one or more of these officers. Match the appointment in column A with the job description in column B. The first one has been done for you as an example.

Column A	Column B
1. Staff Officer (SO)	a. I act as personal assistant to the general.
2. Quartermaster (QM)	b. I direct close air support.
3. Public Relations Officer (PRO)	c. I assist the battalion commander with his administrative work.
4. Aide-de-camp (ADC)	d. I work in a brigade headquarters.
5. Forward Air Controller (FAC)	e. I command a company-sized grouping of artillery.
6. Commanding Officer (CO)	f. I am responsible for coordinating staff duties within the battalion headquarters.
7. Intelligence Officer (IO)	g. I command a company.
8. Liaison Officer (LO)	h. I deal with the media.
9. Forward Observation Officer (FOO)	i. I direct artillery fire.
10. Battery Commander (BC)	j. I am responsible for the logistics of the battalion.
11. Ammunition Technical Officer (ATO)	k. I collect and analyse information about the enemy.
12. Executive Officer (XO)	l. I command a battalion.
13. Officer Commanding (OC)	m. I act as a link between the brigade and the battle groups.
14. Adjutant	n. I dispose of unexploded bombs.

Extension: Work with a partner to write descriptions of appointments within your unit.

Orders 1

British and American ground forces use the the same set of headings for preparing their operational orders.

This format can be applied to any type of operation.

A. Ground.

B. Situation. **i. Enemy Forces.**
ii. Friendly Forces.
ii. Attachments and Detachments.

C. Mission.

D. Execution. **i. Concept of Operations.**
ii. Detailed Tasks.
iii. Coordinating Instructions.

E. Administration and Logistics.

F. Command and Signal.

C Company is about to take part in a battalion attack. The sentences below have been extracted from the company commander's orders. Match each sentence to the correct heading (and sub-heading if necessary). The first one has been done for you as an example.

1. The objective is occupied by elements of the 3rd Airborne Division. B i
2. If I am hit, Capt Thomas will take over until the 2IC arrives. ______
3. 9 Platoon's objective is the church at grid 424719. ______
4. C Company will capture the village of Pratzen. ______
5. The company will assault with two platoons forward and one in reserve. ______
6. H-Hour is at 0415 hours. ______
7. The surrounding area is open farmland. ______
8. B Company will be on our left. Their objective is the wood at grid 440720. ______
9. Each man will carry four anti-personnel grenades and one smoke grenade. ______
10. Our frequency is 0475 MHz. ______
11. G40D is attached to company headquarters for the attack. ______
12. Requests for indirect fire support will be made through G40D. ______
13. The RAP is at grid 435715. ______
14. Hunt Ball means that the objective is secure. ______

Extension. Write your own set of orders for an imaginary operation.

Offensive and defensive operations

Exercise 1
Some verbs are associated primarily with offensive operations, while others are more usually associated with defence. Look at the verbs below and put them in the relevant columns. The first one has been done for you as an example.

~~advance~~ • attack • capture • counter-attack • delay
deny • envelop • fortify • hold • outflank

Offence
advance

Defence

Exercise 2
Now complete each sentence, using one of the verbs above. You may have to change the form of the verb to fit the grammar of the sentence.

1. We were still reorganizing on the objective when the enemy ______________ .
2. The enemy are trying to ______________ us on the left.
3. 7 Corps is ______________ towards Minden.
4. Our mission is to ______________ the enemy until the other battle groups have crossed the river.
5. The brigade ______________ its positions until 1030 hours. Then it was forced to withdraw.
6. The enemy has ______________ B Company. They are now completely cut off.
7. We must ______________ these routes to the enemy for as long as possible.
8. We were unable to support the Fusiliers as they ______________ the village of Landshut.
9. Enemy paratroopers have ______________ the bridge at Arnheim.
10. We had just finished ______________ our positions when we came under fire.

Combined operations

Most large-scale military operations involve a high level of cooperation between the different arms and services. It is therefore essential for all servicemen to have a wide vocabulary of military terms and expressions.

Below is a report written about an imaginary combined arms operation. Use the words and expressions from the box to fill in the gaps in the text.

air defence • naval gunfire support • line of defence • beachhead naval bombardment • Engineer • sorties • airborne • deliberate attack forward observation officer • close air support • landing craft

REPORT

Combined arms operation

On D-1, (1)____________________ units were dropped by parachute to seize strategic crossings over the River Dingwezi. All of these objectives were achieved, with minimal loss. The beach landings on D-Day were preceded by an intensive (2)____________________ , which failed to silence all of the enemy coastal batteries. Consequently, ten percent of the (3)____________________ in the first wave were either destroyed or disabled. Despite this, all primary objectives were achieved by 1100 hours, although ground forces continued to rely upon (4)____________________ until the artillery had been fully offloaded. (5)____________________ units suffered particularly high casualties in the breaching of a secondary line of obstacles in the sand dunes. The (6)____________________ was fully established by 1900 hours on D-Day. The main enemy force has withdrawn to the River Muzenga and is now constructing a strong (7)____________________ between Tangji and Leopoldsville. To date, carrier-based strike aircraft have flown a total of 82 (8)____________________. The enemy (9)____________________ has been better than anticipated, and 8 allied aircraft have been shot down. Owing to a shortage of forward air controllers, most (10)____________________ has been directed by (11)____________________ from the artillery. The 4th and 7th Armoured Brigades started crossing the River Dingwezi at 1030 hours on D+1 and are now preparing to mount a (12)____________________ on the Muzenga position at first light on D+2.

Don't forget to keep a record of the words and expressions that you have learnt, review your notes from time to time and try to use new vocabulary items whenever possible.

Radio conversations

The lines in these radio conversations are in the wrong order. Work out the correct order and write the sequence in the boxes. The first line of each conversation has been done for you as an example.

Conversation 1

☐ 1, confirm grid 820049. Over.

☐ 11, correct. We have three casualties. Two walking wounded and one stretcher case. Roger so far? Over.

1 Hello 1, this is 11. Request casevac at grid 820049. Over.

☐ 1, roger. Out.

☐ 1, roger. Over.

☐ 11, LZ will be marked with blue smoke. Over.

Conversation 2

☐ 2, roger. Move now to grid 479431. Over.

☐ 22, send. Over.

☐ 22, say again grid. Over.

☐ 2, when you get there, go firm and wait for 44C to join you. Then continue with your task. Over.

☐ 22, grid 481428. Over.

☐ 2, grid 479431. Over.

☐ 2, what is your location? Over.

☐ 22, roger. Over.

1 Hello 22, this is 2. Over.

☐ 22, wilco. Out.

Extension. Practise the conversations with a partner.

Commands and warnings

When you are operating with English-speaking troops, it is essential that you understand the various commands and warnings which are used. Your life may depend upon it!

Match the terms and phrases in column A to their correct definitions in column B. The first one has been done for you as an example.

Column A	Column B
1. Make ready!	a. Get into a lifeboat; the vessel is about to sink .
2. Take cover!	b. A chemical agent has just been used.
3. Unload!	c. Shoot as quickly as possible (infantry).
4. Halt!	d. Cock your weapon.
5. Tank action!	e. The enemy has been sighted.
6. Open fire!	f. Shoot as quickly as possible (artillery or mortars).
7. Gas! Gas! Gas!	g. Find yourself some protection from enemy fire.
8. Fire for effect!	h. Stop moving and adopt a position of defence.
9. Go firm!	i. Get out of your vehicle.
10. Cease fire!	j. Remove the magazine from the weapon and check that the breech is clear of ammunition. Pull the trigger and apply the safety catch, then replace the magazine on the weapon.
11. Abandon ship!	k. Start shooting.
12. Debus!	l. Fire one round, so that the fall of shot can be observed (artillery or mortars).
13. Rapid fire!	m. Go to your battle position immediately.
14. Make safe!	n. Remove all ammunition from the weapon and ensure that it is clear.
15. Incoming!	o. Prepare to engage armoured vehicles.
16. Action stations!	p. Stop shooting.
17. Adjust fire!	q. Stop moving immediately.
18. Contact!	r. Shells are about to land on our position.

Orders 2

Sheet A

Work with a partner who has sheet B. You are a platoon commander and your call-sign is 31L.

When the point platoon (call-sign 32) came under fire, the company commander went forward on foot to recce the enemy position. He also came under heavy fire and cannot move back, but he has just sent orders on the radio for a quick attack. Because of the noise, you did not hear all the details. Talk to the other platoon commander (call-sign 33L) and try to fill in the gaps by asking questions.

Follow these two rules: 1. Speak only English.
2. Don't show your sheet to your partner until you have finished.

GROUND:

- **The objective** is a farm on the ridge, at grid 481245.
  There are buildings on both sides of the road.
  At grid 480241 there is a crossroads, which is in dead ground to the farm.
  This will be ______________________________ .

SITUATION:

- **Enemy Forces:** The enemy is in the farm.
  Their strength is ______________ , but they have two ATGW firing posts and at least two medium machine guns.

- **Friendly Forces:** 32 are at grid ______________ . They have lost one vehicle.
  Sunray is at grid ______________________________ .

MISSION:

- To clear the enemy from the farm at grid 481245.

EXECUTION:

- **Concept of Operations:** This attack will be made on foot.
  31 and 33 will ______________________________ ,
  using the road as their axis.
  The move to the FUP will be covered by smoke.
  32 will ______________________________ .
  The vehicles will stay where they are until called forward.

- **Detailed Tasks:**
  31 - clear the buildings on the right of the road.
  32 - ______________________________ .
  33 - clear the buildings on the left of the road.

- **Coordinating Instructions:**
  Indirect Fire Support: 10 minutes of smoke on the objective, starting at 1425 hours.
  Timings: 1425 - Smoke on the objective. Assault group move to the FUP.
  H-Hour - ______________________________ .
  Route to FUP: Move to grid ____________________ , then follow the road up to the crossroads.

ADMINISTRATION AND LOGISTICS:

- **No change.**

COMMAND AND SIGNAL:

- **Command:** __________ will command the assault group. 31M will now command 31.

Orders 2

Sheet B

Work with a partner who has sheet A. You are a platoon commander and your call-sign is 33L.

When the point platoon (call-sign 32) came under fire, the company commander went forward on foot to recce the enemy position. He also came under heavy fire and cannot move back, but he has just sent orders on the radio for a quick attack. Because of the noise, you did not hear all the details. Talk to the other platoon commander (call-sign 31L) and try to fill in the gaps by asking questions.

Follow these two rules: 1. Speak only English.
2. Don't show your sheet to your partner until you have finished.

GROUND:

- **The objective** is a farm on the ridge, at grid 481245. There are buildings on both sides of the road.

  At grid 480241 there is ____________________ , which is in dead ground to the farm. This will be the FUP.

SITUATION:

- **Enemy Forces:** The enemy is in the farm.
  Their strength is not known, but they have ______________________________
  ____
  ____ .

- **Friendly Forces:** 32 are at grid 478240. They have lost ____________________ Sunray is at grid 480239.

MISSION:

- ____ .

EXECUTION:

- **Concept of Operations:** This attack will be ______________ 31 and 33 will make a frontal assault on the farm, using the road as their axis. The move to the FUP will be ______________ 32 will provide fire support from their present position. The vehicles will ______________________________ .

- **Detailed Tasks:**

  31 - clear the buildings on the right of the road.

  32 - provide fire support until the assault reaches the farm, then move up to the objective.

  33 - ____ .

- **Coordinating Instructions:**

  Indirect Fire Support: ____ .

  Timings: 1425 - Smoke on the objective. Assault group move to the FUP.
  H-Hour - as soon as the assault group is formed up.

  Route to FUP: Move to grid 482241, then ______________________________ .

ADMINISTRATION AND LOGISTICS:

- **No change.**

COMMAND AND SIGNAL:

- **Command:** 31L will command the assault group. 31M will now command 31.

Abbreviations

Test your abbreviations. What do the following stand for? The first one has been done for you as an example.

1. FUP ______ *forming-up point* ______
2. NCO ______
3. QRF ______
4. NGS ______
5. HF ______
6. UN ______
7. LMG ______
8. MAW ______
9. ETA ______
10. VCP ______
11. MFC ______
12. KIA ______
13. AWLS ______
14. NBC ______
15. CAP ______
16. GMT ______
17. OOB ______
18. PT ______
19. SOP ______
20. FGA ______
21. STOVL ______
22. IR ______
23. ERA ______
24. TEWT ______
25. FTX ______

Extension: work with a partner to test one another. One person closes the book, while the other asks questions such as *"What does FUP stand for?"*

British and American English 1

British and American service men sometimes spell or write words differently. Look at the pairs of words below. Write the British version in column A and its American equivalent on the opposite side in column B. The first pair has been done for you as an example.

color / colour • haemorrhage / hemorrhage • kilometer / kilometre
pickax / pickaxe • armour / armor • lieutenant colonel / lieutenant - colonel
signaller / signaler • manoeuvre / maneuver • epaulet / epaulette
harbour / harbor • fireteam / fire team • defence / defense
Alfa / Alpha • reconnoitre / reconnoiter • Whisky / Whiskey

Column A (British)	Column B (American)
colour	color

Extension:
Work with a partner to test one another, using the phonetic alphabet. For example:

Question: ***What is the American spelling of colour?***
Answer: ***Charlie - Oscar - Lima - Oscar - Romeo***

British and American English 2

British and American servicemen sometimes use different words and expressions to talk about the same thing.

Look at the words and expressions below. Half of them are British and half are the American equivalents. Identify the pairs and then write the British word or expression in column A, and its American equivalent on the opposite side in column B. One pair has been done for you as an example.

NAAFI • ~~furlough~~ • gasoline • lock and load • int • petrol • foxhole
bearing • PX • ~~leave~~ • recon • squad • fire-trench • section
Staballoy • make ready • azimuth • depleted uranium • intel • recce

Column A (British)	Column B (American)
leave	furlough

Extension:
Work with a partner to test one another by asking questions such as:

"What is the British equivalent of furlough? "

Slang

Most professions develop their own peculiar vocabulary of slang words and the services are no exception. The sentences below each contain one example of military slang. Underline the slang words and then match them to the definitions in the column on the right. The first one has been done for you as an example.

Sentences containing military slang:	Definitions:
a. What is that ***civvy*** doing here?	1. Infantryman ______
b. We've liberated three bottles of slivovitz from that deserted farmhouse.	2. To deliberately wound a comrade, giving the appearance that he was hit by enemy fire ______
c. The shell exploded as the men were lining up for chow.	3. To steal ______
d. I met him while I was still a rookie.	4. To destroy ______
e. He got zapped by a sniper this morning.	5. To shoot someone dead ______
f. Watch out! There's a bandit on your tail!	6. Disorderly behaviour leading to violence ______
g. I requested a transfer from the Guards, because I couldn't take all the bull.	7. Someone who is not a member of the armed forces civvy
h. There is a rumour going around that Sergeant Ellis was fragged during the bombardment.	8. Food ______
i. We took out the lead tank as it was crossing the railway line.	9. Cleaning and polishing kit ______
j. He is going to be an instructor at boot camp.	10. Recruit ______
k. The grunts always get the dirty jobs.	11. Training establishment for new recruits ______
l. We're expecting aggro tonight, so bring plenty of baton rounds.	12. Enemy fighter aircraft ______

Armoured fighting vehicles

Test your AFV recognition. Match the vehicle types in the box with the silhouettes below.

armoured personnel carrier • main battle tank • self-propelled gun infantry fighting vehicle • light tank • armoured car multiple rocket launcher • self-propelled anti-aircraft gun

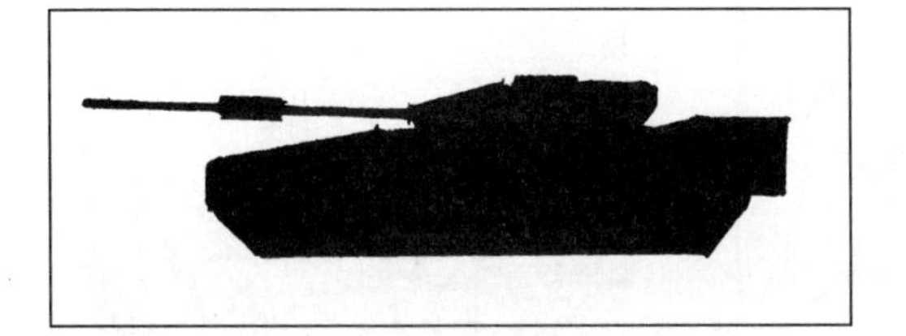

1.________________________________

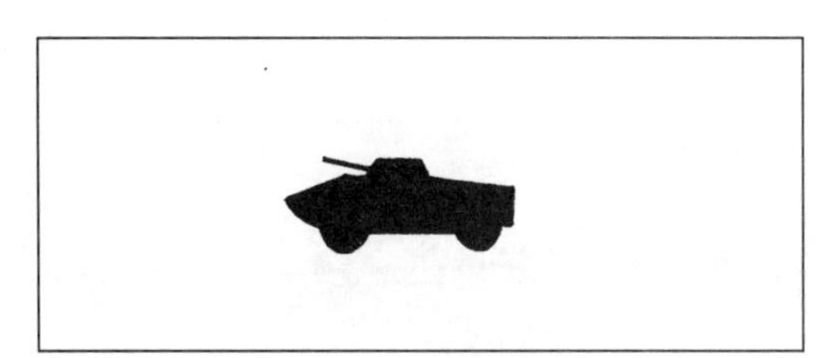

2.________________________________

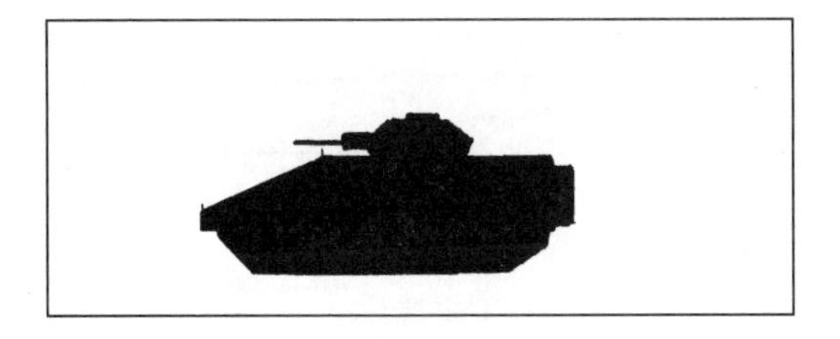

3.________________________________

4.________________________________

5.________________________________

6.________________________________

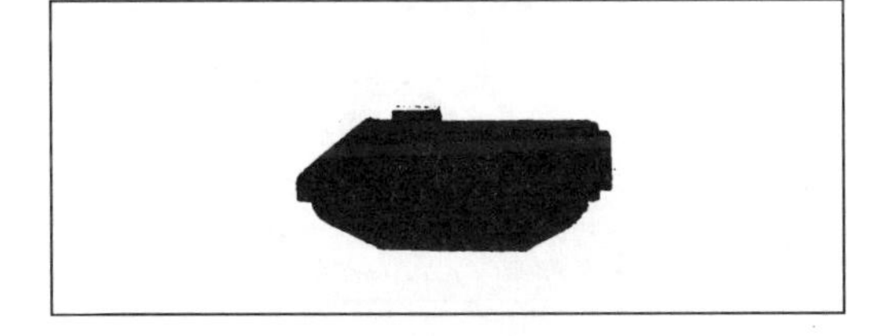

7.________________________________

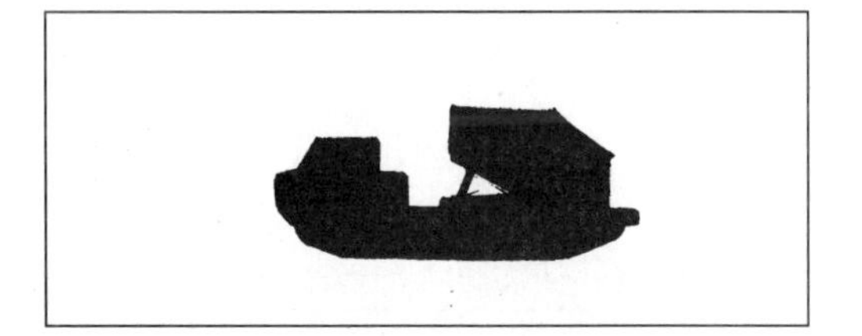

8.________________________________

Positions and locations

Match the terms in the box with the pictures below.

POL point • dressing station • vehicle check-point • ammunition dump fire-trench • firing post • bunker • command post • LZ

1. ____________________

2. ____________________

3. ____________________

4. ____________________

5. ____________________

6. ____________________

7. ____________________

8. ____________________

9. ____________________

Categories 1: armoured fighting vehicles

In this table there are 18 armoured fighting vehicles and five categories of vehicle. Decide which category each vehicle belongs to. The first one has been done for you as an example.

	MBT	IFV	APC	SPG	CVR
Abbot				X	
Abrams					
AFV-432					
AMX-30					
BMP					
Bradley					
BRDM					
BTR-80					
Challenger					
Leopard					
M-113					
M-109					
M-1974					
Marder					
MT-LB					
Scimitar					
T-72					
Warrior					

Extension: Work with a partner to produce further examples of each category.

Categories 2: aircraft

In this table there are 18 aircraft and four categories of aircraft. Decide which category each aircraft belongs to. The first one has been done for you as an example.

	Fighter	Bomber	Attack Helicopter	Utility/Transport Helicopter
Apache			X	
Backfire				
Blackhawk				
Chinook				
Cobra				
Eagle				
Flanker				
Flogger				
Hind				
Hip				
Hook				
Huey				
Lancer				
Mirage				
Phantom				
Puma				
Spirit				
Tomcat				

Extension: Work with a partner to produce further examples of each category.

Categories 3: missiles

In this table there are 18 missiles and four categories of missile. Decide which category each missile belongs to. The first one has been done for you as an example.

	ATGW	SAM	AAM	Anti-ship
AMRAAM			**X**	
Aphid				
Blowpipe				
Exocet				
Gaskin				
Grail				
Harpoon				
Kormoran				
Milan				
Rapier				
Sagger				
Sea Eagle				
Sea Wolf				
Sidewinder				
Sky Flash				
Spandrel				
Stinger				
TOW				

Extension: Work with a partner to produce further examples of each category.

Communicative crossword 1

Sheet A

This crossword is not complete: you only have half the words. The other half are on sheet B. Check that you know the words in your crossword. Then work with a partner who has sheet B to complete the two crosswords.

Follow these three rules:

1. **Speak only in English.**
2. **Don't say the word in the crossword.**
3. **Don't show your crossword to your partner.**

" What's 1 across ? "
→ across ↓ down

YOUR NOTES

Communicative crossword 1

Sheet B

This crossword is not complete: you only have half the words. The other half are on sheet A. Check that you know the words in your crossword. Then work with a partner who has sheet A to complete the two crosswords.

Follow these three rules:

1. **Speak only in English.**
2. **Don't say the word in the crossword.**
3. **Don't show your crossword to your partner.**

" What's 1 across ? "
→ across ↓ down

[1] A	M	M	[2] U	N	I	[3] T	I	O	[4] N	■	[5]			[6]
M	■	■		■	■	R	■	■	E	■	■	■	■	
B	■	■		■	■	A	■	■	[7] T	R	[8] E	N	C	H
U	■	■	[9] I	N	D	I	A	■	■	■		■	■	
[10] S				■	■	N	■	[11] I	■	[12]			■	
H	■	■	[13] E	[14] N	S	I	G	N	■	■		■	■	
■	■	[15] A	■	E	■	N	■	[16] T	I	D	E	■	■	■
■	■	R	■	U	■	G	■	E	■	■	[17]			[18]
[19] R	E	M	O	T	E	■	■	[20] R		[21]	■	■	■	
E	■	■	■	R	■	■	■	V	■		■	[22]	■	
[23] G		[24]		A			■	E	■		■		■	
U	■		■	L	■	■	■	N	■		■		■	
L	■		■	[25] I		[26] S		E						■
A	■		■	Z	■	E	■	■	■		■		■	■
[27] R	E	T	R	E	A	T	■	■	[28]					

YOUR NOTES

Word search

Find the 23 military terms hidden in the letters below; 10 read across and 13 read down. The first word has been found for you as an example. The clues listed beneath will help you to find all the words.

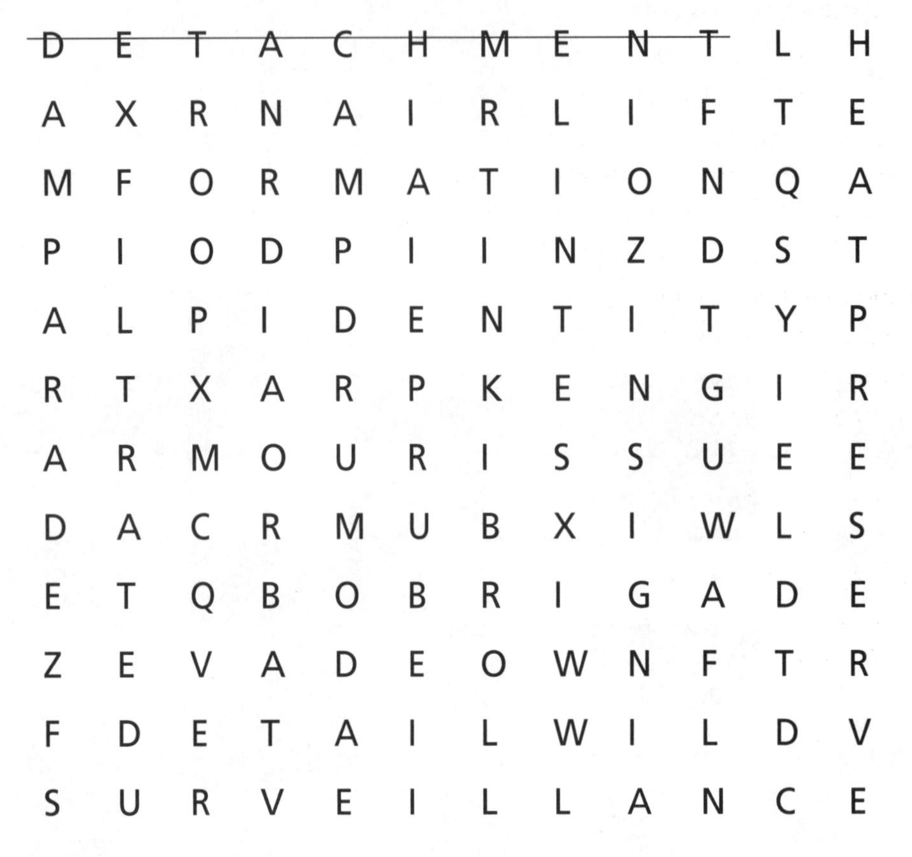

1. Small administrative or tactical grouping.
2. Official list of personnel in a unit or sub-unit.
3. Metal container used to store food over long periods.
4. Defensive covering designed to protect a vehicle from bullets or shrapnel.
5. Arrangement of aircraft, ships, troops or vehicles for tactical purposes.
6. Action of assembling at a specific time and place.
7. Units or sub-units which are held back from an engagement so that they can be used as reinforcements.
8. Who a person is.
9. Small group of soldiers assigned to carry out a specific task.
10. To withdraw in small groups and by different routes through enemy-controlled territory.
11. To supply a person or unit with equipment.
12. Cylindrical container.
13. Decorative symbol.
14. Amount of explosive power produced by a nuclear weapon.
15. Place where people are accomodated in temporary shelter.
16. Tactical grouping of two or more battalions or regiments.
17. Any method which can be used to locate or observe the enemy or listen to their radio transmissions.
18. Platoon-sized armoured grouping.
19. Movement of men or equipment or supplies using aircraft.
20. Order of Battle (abbreviation).
21. Type of anti-tank warhead.
22. To take avoiding action.
23. Information obtained by monitoring the enemy's electronic transmissions.

Anagrams

Solve the anagrams by reading the clues and putting the letters in to form words. Enter the solutions in the table to find the mystery term. The first one has been done for you as an example.

1. To meet up with someone as he moves from one place to another ____________ RTTEIPNEC
2. Light fast-moving aircraft designed to attack other aircraft ____________ FRITGHE
3. Tactical grouping of three or more platoons ____________ OPMNACY
4. Cattle disease used as a biological weapon ____________ HTNAARX
5. Incident where two forces shoot at each other ____________ REIFIFHGT
6. Prolonged engagement involving large numbers of troops ____________ TTABEL
7. Specific task assigned to a tactical grouping ____________ NOSIMIS
8. Method by which 7 (above) is carried out ____________ TENOCIEUX
9. Armoured equivalent of 3 (above) ____________ DUQSANOR
10. Use of natural and man-made materials to disguise an object. ____________ GUOMAFELAC
11. Assistance or help ____________ UTSPROP
12. Projectiles formed by fragments of an exploding shell ____________ PANSHLER
13. Serviceman who specializes in the use of radios ____________ LANGLISGER
14. Artillery attack (usually lasting some time) ____________ NOBEBRDTAMBM
15. Designed to set things on fire ____________ YIIERNDCAN
16. American-designed surface-to-air missile ____________ GINTERS

Mystery term clue: used for spelling on the radio

Military trivia 1

See how many of these questions you can answer.

1. Who is more senior? A lieutenant-general or a major-general? ______
2. What is the nickname of the American F-4 fighter aircraft? ______
3. What is a Kalashnikov? ______
4. What is Fuller's earth used for ? ______
5. What is Semtex? ______
6. Which service of the British armed forces is senior? The army or the navy? ______
7. What does ASAP mean? ______
8. How do you convert a grid bearing into a magnetic bearing ? ______
9. There are 360 degrees in a circle. How many mils are there? ______
10. What is Kevlar? ______
11. What is scrim? ______
12. Which is bigger? A division or a brigade? ______
13. What is the equivalent of the Red Cross in Islamic countries? ______
14. What does starboard mean? ______
15. What is the main weapon on a British Scimitar light tank? ______
16. What does MASH mean? ______
17. What is a padre? ______
18. What is the American equivalent of a British air vice marshal? ______
19. What is a kukri? ______
20. How fast is one knot? ______

Communicative crossword 2

Sheet A

This crossword is not complete: you only have half the words. The other half are on sheet B. Check that you know the words in your crossword. Then work with a partner who has sheet B to complete the two crosswords.

Follow these three rules:

1. **Speak only in English.**
2. **Don't say the word in the crossword.**
3. **Don't show your crossword to your partner.**

" What's 1 across ? "
→ across ↓ down

1						2 G		■	3 R	A	4 T	I	O	5 N
	■	■	■	■	■	U	■	■	■	■	O	■	■	E
6 I	L	7 L	U	8 M	I	N	A	T	9 E	■	10 W	11		G
	■	A	■		■	N	■	■	S	■	■		■	L
12		S				E	■	■	T	■	■	G	■	I
	■	E	■		■	R	■	13	I					G
	■	R	■		■	■	■	■	M	■	■		■	E
	■	■	14			■	■	15 C	A	P	T	A	I	N
■	■	16 A	■		■	■	■	■	T	■	■		■	C
17		R			18 G	■	■	19 R	E	L	I	E	V	E
	■	E	■	■	L	■	■	■	■	■	■	■	■	■
20 F	R	A	21 T	R	I	C	I	D	E	■	22	■	■	23 W
	■	■	R	■	D	■	■	■	■	24				A
	■	■	A	■	E	■	■	■	■	■		■	■	R
25			P		R			■	26 C	O	R	D	O	N

YOUR NOTES

Communicative crossword 2

Sheet B

This crossword is not complete: you only have half the words. The other half are on sheet A. Check that you know the words in your crossword. Then work with a partner who has sheet A to complete the two crosswords.

Follow these three rules:

1. **Speak only in English.**
2. **Don't say the word in the crossword.**
3. **Don't show your crossword to your partner.**

" What's 1 across ? "
→ across ↓ down

1 S	A	B	O	T	A	2 G	E		3		4			5
K														
6 I		7		8 M					9		10 W	11 I	N	G
R				A								N		
12 M	I	S	S	I	L	E						D		
I				N				13 M	I	S	S	I	N	G
S				T								C		
H			14 M	A	P			15				A		
		16		I								T		
17 D	A	R	I	N	18 G			19				E		
E														
20 F			21								22 R			23
E										24 M	E	D	I	A
N											A			
25 D	I	S	P	E	R	S	E		26		R			

YOUR NOTES

Anagrams 2

Solve the anagrams by reading the clues and putting the letters in to form words. Enter the solutions in the table to find the mystery term. The first one has been done for you as an example.

1. Rotary-wing aircraft ____________ CTIPOLHERE
2. Act of destroying a structure ____________ NTOLMIODEI
3. To move towards the enemy ____________ CAVDENA
4. Opposite of 3 (above) ____________ RIHTWWAD
5. Power source for portable electrical equipment ____________ TYBARET
6. Type of fuel ____________ INSAGOEL
7. Relating to infantry equipped with APCs ____________ DIZHCEEMAN
8. To be able to shoot further than another weapon ____________ GETUOANR
9. Most senior person in a grouping ____________ MADNOMECR
10. Warship designed to move and operate under water ____________ MUSARNIBE
11. Orders or instructions ____________ GREBIFIN
12. Power to direct the actions of people or things ____________ LONRTOC
13. Type of warship ____________ RYOSDERTE
14. Danger ____________ SISSDRET

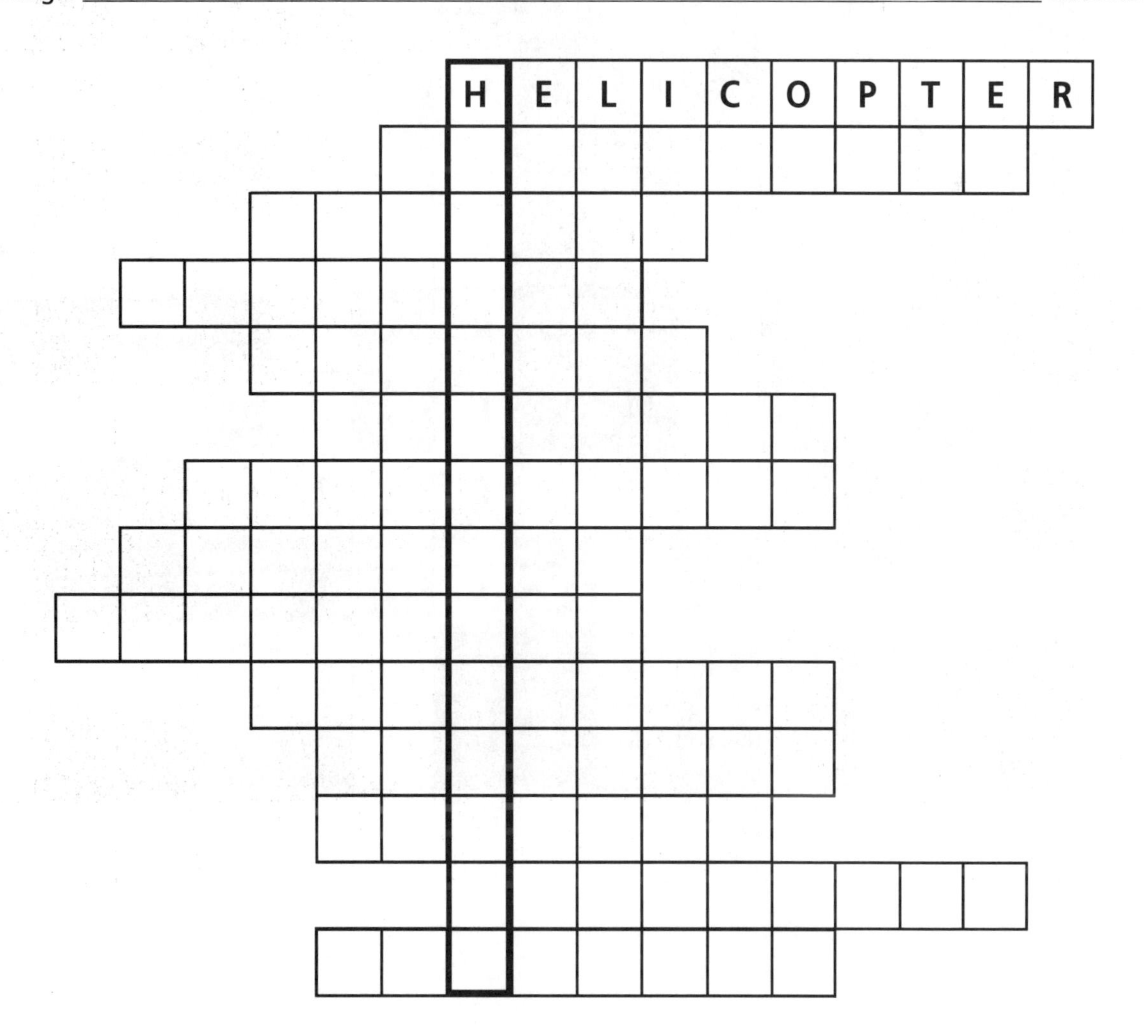

Mystery term clue: philosophy of winning the support of the civilian population

Communicative crossword 3

Sheet A

This crossword is not complete: you only have half the words. The other half are on sheet B. Check that you know the words in your crossword. Then work with a partner who has sheet B to complete the two crosswords.

Follow these three rules:

1. **Speak only in English.**
2. **Don't say the word in the crossword.**
3. **Don't show your crossword to your partner.**

" What's 1 across ? "
→ across ↓ down

1 P	Y	2 R	O	T	E	3 C	H	N	I	4 C		5		6 G
A		U												E
R		B		7										N
8 A	M	B	U	L	A	N	C	E						E
P		L							9 M	U	S	T	E	R
10 E		E	11					12 C						A
T					13 A			O						L
	14				L			15 R	E	C	O	I	L	
16					E			R						
					R			E				17		18
		19 R	E	20 S	T	21 R	I	C	T	E	D			
		O				A		T						
		U				D			22					
		N				A								
23 R	A	D	I	O		24 R	E	S	E	R	V	O	I	R

YOUR NOTES

Communicative crossword 3

Sheet B

This crossword is not complete: you only have half the words. The other half are on sheet A. Check that you know the words in your crossword. Then work with a partner who has sheet A to complete the two crosswords.

Follow these three rules:

1. **Speak only in English.**
2. **Don't say the word in the crossword.**
3. **Don't show your crossword to your partner.**

" What's 1 across ? "
→ across ↓ down

1		2				3 C				4 C	■	5 L	O	6 G
	■		■	■	■	R	■	■	■	O	■	O	■	
	■		■	7 A	■	A	■	■	■	M	■	C	■	
8				L		N			■	M	■	A	■	
	■		■	L	■	E	■	■	9	U		T		
10 E	N	E	11 M	Y	■	■	■	12	■	N	■	E	■	
	■	■	A	■	13	■	■		■	I	■	■	■	
■	14 M	O	R	A	L	E	■	15		C				■
16 T	■	■	I	■		■	■		■	A	■	■	■	■
R	■	■	N	■		■	■		■	T	■	17 M	I	18 L
A	■	19	E	20 S		21				E		■	■	O
I	■		■	A	■		■		■	■	■	■	■	O
L	■		■	L	■		■	■	22 I	N	D	E	N	T
E	■		■	V	■		■	■	C	■	■	■	■	E
23 R				O	■	24			E					R

YOUR NOTES

Military trivia 2

See how many of these questions you can answer.

1. What does reveille mean?____________________

2. What is a bowser? ____________________

3. What is the twelfth letter of the phonetic alphabet? ____________________

4. What are dragon's teeth?____________________

5. What does C-in-C mean ? ____________________

6. What are caltrops?____________________

7. What is the nickname of the American UH-1 utility helicopter? ____________________

8. What is the main role of a hunter-killer submarine? ____________________

9. What is the name of the officers' mess on a warship?____________________

10. What is a Jolly Green Giant? ____________________

11. What is no-man's-land?____________________

12. What is an iron bomb? ____________________

13. What is flak?____________________

14. What is the mechanism which prevents a weapon from being fired? ____________________

15. What does neutral mean?____________________

16. What is a pontoon bridge? ____________________

17. What does FLOT mean?____________________

18. What is a Molotov cocktail?____________________

19. What is the chief of staff in a British brigade usually called?____________________

20. What is the name of the national headquarters of the United States Department of Defence?

____

Military crossword

All the answers in this crossword are connected with military matters.

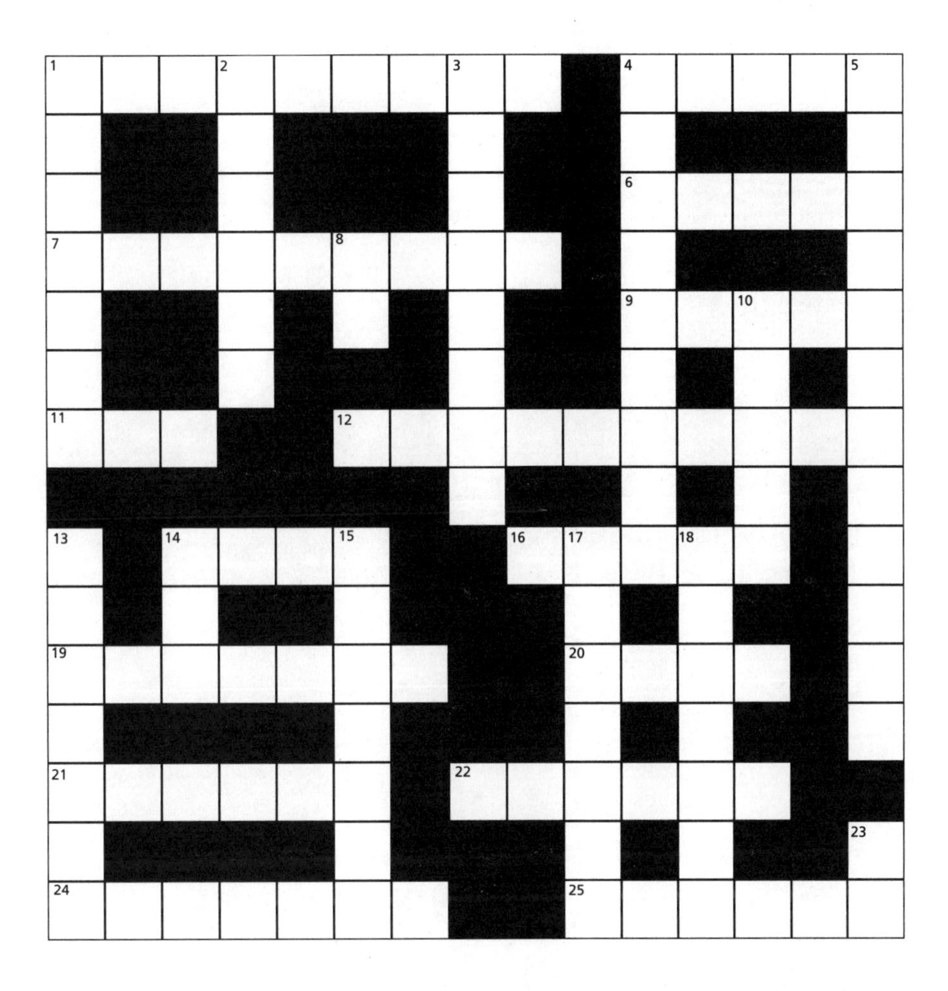

Across

1. Place where food is prepared.
4. System for detecting underwater objects through the transmission of sound waves
6. Company-sized grouping in an American armored cavalry regiment.
7. Act of moving people or things by aircraft, ships or vehicles.
9. First letter of the phonetic alphabet.
11. Battalion casualty clearing-station.
12. One of a series of two-digit numbers shown on a map grid.
14. Exercise involving only the command elements of a tactical grouping.
16. Area of ground used for shooting practice.
19. Defeat of an enemy in battle or war.
20. Armoured fighting vehicle.
21. Specified period of time before something happens.
22. Device which is designed to detect something.
24. Act of taking avoiding action.
25. To act offensively against an enemy.

Down

1. Line on a map connecting points of equal altitude.
2. Accomodation for dogs.
3. British-designed light tank.
4. What is happening at a particular time.
5. People or things which take the place of other people or things.
8. Shopping centre on an American base.
10. State of not being involved in a war.
13. Early.
14. Small mobile battlefield headquarters.
15. Underwater missile designed to explode when it hits a ship.
17. Metal rod, mast or structure used in the transmission of radio signals.
18. Small vessel with heavy guns designed to operate in shallow waters.
23. Adverb meaning 'all right'.

Vocabulary record sheet

Word	Class	Notes, translation, definition, example...

Answer key

WORD BUILDING

Word association 1: missing links (p. 1)

1. support
2. ground
3. grid
4. mine
5. general
6. fire

Two-word expressions (p. 2)

1. home defence
2. exclusion zone
3. compassionate leave
4. voice procedure
5. distress signal
6. observation post
7. supply dump
8. static line
9. pincer movement
10. harrassing fire
11. flight path
12. manoeuvre warfare
13. field gun
14. shock action

Word formation: nouns (p. 3)

1. The enemy advance has reached Reichenbach
2. We should expect a loss in aircraft of at least ten percent.
3. The enemy withdrawal started at last light.
4. I will arrange recovery of the vehicle.
5. The attack was made under cover of smoke.
6. The registration of all targets must be completed by 1600 hours.
7. The landing of the troops will take place at night.
8. The destruction of the bridge delayed the reinforcements.
9. The flight to Cyprus took seven hours.
10. We were not informed about their retreat.
11. The route clearance is still going on.
12. 6 Platoon will carry out a reconnaissance of the enemy position.

Word marriages: nouns (p. 4)

1. lifeboat
2. breakthrough
3. minefield
4. ceasefire
5. warhead
6. waypoint
7. searchlight
8. guardroom
9. footbridge
10. foghorn
11. roadblock
12. countermeasure

Word association (2): partnerships (p. 5)

1. first aid
2. chemical agent
3. multinational force
4. collateral damage
5. thermal image
6. classified information
7. stealth bomber
8. negligent discharge
9. high-velocity bullet
10. interior lines
11. corrugated iron
12. air photograph

Three-word expressions (p. 6)

1. forward air controller
2. immediate action drill
3. inter-continental ballistic missile
4. improvised explosive device
5. general deployment position
6. post-traumatic stress disorder
7. remotely piloted vehicle
8. final protective fire
9. laser target designator
10. primary aircraft authorized
11. joint task force
12. foreign object damage

Word association (3) mind maps (p. 7)

1. G4
2. TAC
3. promotion
4. staff
5. personnel
6. intelligence
7. operations
8. orders
9. SIGINT
10. exercise

PARTS OF SPEECH

Nouns (1) (p. 8)

1. password
2. interdiction
3. pillbox
4. northing
5. O Group
6. fallout
7. frontage
8. trace
9. fireplan
10. wreckage
11. flagship
12. intsum
13. demolition
14. riot
15. resistance

Nouns (2) (p. 9)

1. T-junction
2. crossroads
3. village
4. church
5. orchard
6. quarry
7. field
8. farm
9. wood
10. hedge
11. castle
12. copse
13. ridge
14. road
15. track
16. knoll
17. lake
18. river
19. railway line
20. bridge
21. town
22. spur
23. re-entrant
24. factory
25. forest
26. hill
27. mountain
28. saddle
29. summit
30. pass

Adjectives (p. 10)

1. secure
2. diversionary
3. non-persistent
4. hostile
5. optical
6. self-propelled
7. incendiary
8. combat-effective
9. subordinate
10. untenable
11. multirole
12. preparatory
13. unserviceable
14. civilian
15. wire-guided

Verbs: present continuous (p. 11)

1. He is briefing
2. They are forming up
3. They are advancing
4. They are debussing
5. They are assaulting
6. The enemy are withdrawing
7. They are reorganizing
8. The enemy are counter-attacking
9. The enemy are retreating

Verbs: present perfect (p. 12)

1. c
2. g
3. f
4. k
5. j
6. m
7. a
8. l
9. n
10. b
11. o
12. h
13. e
14. d
15. i

Answer key

Verbs: mixed tenses (p. 13)

1. interrogated
2. intercepted
3. strafed
4. insert
5. commandeer
6. jammed
7. suppressed
8. deploying
9. camouflaging
10. bridged
11. mask
12. replenished
13. arm
14. shelling
15. relieve

Verbs: active / passive (p. 14)

1. Three enemy fighters were shot down during the battle.
2. Last night the Chief of Police was assassinated.
3. The weapons were concealed in an old oil drum.
4. HMS Brilliant has been sunk by a torpedo.
5. The bridge at Zemun has been blown.
6. The airfield has been captured.
7. B Company is being shelled.
8. The convoy was ambushed by partisans as it was moving through the gorge.
9. The minefield has been breached.
10. Our radio transmissions are being intercepted.
11. Our tanks are outranged by the enemy.
12. Our OP has been compromised.

Phrasal verbs (1) (p. 15)

1. d
2. i
3. f
4. k
5. j
6. a
7. e
8. l
9. c
10. g
11. o
12. b
13. h
14. m
15. n

Phrasal verbs (2) (p. 16)

1. took off
2. lay up
3. digging in
4. roll up
5. homed in
6. bug out
7. gave up
8. picked up
9. fell in
10. held out
11. push on
12. bombing up
13. stood to
14. standing by
15. mopping up

Prepositions (p. 17)

1. He is currently based ~~at~~ ^ Germany. *in*
2. Load ~~by~~ ^ sabot ! *with*
3. We debussed in front ^ the enemy position. *of*
4. They only have enough rounds ~~to~~ ^ one more fire mission. *for*
5. A Company captured ~~of~~ their objective thirty minutes ago.
6. The second ^ command is Major Bunbury. *in*
7. H-Hour is ~~on~~ ^ 0545 hours. *at*
8. We were unable ^ recover the damaged vehicle. *to*
9. We moved to the exercise area ~~with~~ ^ bus. *by*
10. He was charged ~~of~~ ^ cowardice. *with*
11. The enemy attacked ~~to~~ B Company's position last night.
12. We came ~~in~~ ^ fire as we were crossing the town square. *under*
13. We've just received a message ~~by~~ ^ Brigade Headquarters. *from*
14. USS Nimitz is already ~~on~~ ^ sea. *at*
15. Captain MacDonald is ~~at~~ ^ leave. *on*

PRONOUNCIATION

Word stress (p. 18)

Group A: area, classified, company, enemy, signaller, radio, exercise, accident.

Group B: commander, established, intentions, preparing, demolish, position, unable, division.

Group C: intercept, overseas, saboteurs, engineers, resupply, disembark, brigadier, countermand.

Present simple (p. 19)

Group A: detects, panics, attacks, drops, halts.

Group B: warns, commands, clears, destroys, controls, flies, issues, arms, tows, digs, scatters, covers.

Group C: discharges, skirmishes, reorganizes, launches, practises, carries, marches, disperses.

Extension:

A: tanks, warrants, minutes, bomblets.

B: obstructions, bombs, drills, roads.

C: duties, passes, forces, trenches.

Past simple / past participle (p. 20)

Group A: based, advanced, crashed, dispersed, launched, missed, dumped, checked.

Group B: killed, mined, used, engaged, resupplied, bombed, delayed, reorganized, moved, towed, covered, aimed, captured.

Group C: assaulted, exploded, guided, sited.

Timings (p. 21)

1. sixteen twenty-five hours
2. zero four hundred hours
3. fifteen forty-five hours
4. zero nine ten hours
5. twenty zero nine hours
6. ten fifty-nine hours
7. thirteen thirty hours
8. eighteen hundred hours
9. zero zero forty-three hours
10. twenty hundred hours
11. zero three zero six hours
12. twenty-one ten hours
13. twenty-two eighteen hours
14. seventeen seventeen hours
15. zero zero zero five hours

VOCABULARY IN CONTEXT

Odd one out (p. 22)

1. *submarine:* the others are all surface vessels
2. *machine-gun:* the others are all indirect-fire weapons
3. *soldier:* the others are all irregular troops
4. *minelayer:* the others all destroy mines
5. *reinforcements:* the others are all materiel
6. *lorry:* the others are all armoured vehicles
7. *hill:* the others are all man-made features
8. *Apache:* the others are all fixed-wing aircraft
9. *colonel:* the others are all naval ranks
10. *HE:* the others are all anti-tank warheads
11. *anthrax:* the others are all chemical agents
12. *B-1:* the others are all stealth aircraft
13. *Fantan:* the others are all Soviet-designed fighters
14. *engineers:* the others are all teeth arms
15. *cannon:* the others are all small arms

Multiple meanings (p. 23)

1. charge
2. line
3. wave
4. pass
5. harbour
6. signal
7. jam
8. orders

Answer key

Opposites (p. 24)

Column A	Column B
enemy - friendly	forces
passive - active	night-viewing device
frontal - flanking	attack
covert - overt	operation
blank - live	ammunition
strategic - tactical	bombing
magnetic - grid	bearing
mobile - static	defence
air-portable - mechanized	infantry
acting - substantive	rank
forward - rear	area
wheeled - tracked	vehicle

What do I do? (p. 25)

1. d 2. j 3. h 4. a 5. b
6. l 7. k 8. m 9. i 10. e
11. n 12. f 13. g 14. c

Orders (1) (p. 26)

1. Bi 2. F 3. Dii 4. C 5. Di
6. Diii 7. A 8. Bii 9. E 10. F
11. Biii 12. Diii 13. E 14. F

Offensive and defensive operations (p. 27)

Exercise 1:
Offence: advance, attack, capture, envelop, outflank
Defence: counter-attack, delay, deny, fortify, hold

Exercise 2:
1. counter-attacked 2. outflank
3. advancing 4. delay
5. held 6. enveloped
7. deny 8. attacked
9. captured 10. fortifying

Combined operations (p. 28)

1. airborne 2. naval bombardment
3. landing craft 4. naval gunfire support
5. Engineer 6. beachhead
7. line of defence 8. sorties
9. air defence 10. close air support
11. forward observation officers
12. deliberate attack

Radio conversations (p. 29)

Conversation 1: 2, 3, 1, 6, 4, 5
Conversation 2: 5, 2, 6, 9, 4, 7, 3, 8, 1, 10

Commands and warnings (p. 30)

1. d 2. g 3. n 4. q 5. o
6. k 7. b 8. f 9. h 10. p
11. a 12. i 13. c 14. j 15. r
16. m 17. l 18. e

Abbreviations (p. 33)

1. forming-up point 2. non-commissioned officer
3. quick reaction force 4. naval gunfire support
5. high frequency 6. United Nations
7. light machine-gun 8. medium anti-tank weapon
9. estimated time of arrival 10. vehicle check-point
11. mortar fire controller 12. killed in action
13. amber warning light system
14. nuclear, biological and chemical
15. combat air patrol
16. Greenwich Mean Time 17. out of bounds
18. physical training
19. standard operating procedure
20. fighter ground-attack
21. short take-off and vertical landing
22. infrared 23. explosive reactive armour
24. tactical exercise without troops
25. field training exercise

British and American English (1) (p. 34)

British:
colour, haemorrhage, kilometre, armour, lieutenant-colonel, signaller, manoeuvre, epaulette, harbour, reconnoitre, defence, pickaxe, Alpha, Whisky, fireteam.

American:
color, hemorrhage, kilometer, armor, lieutenant colonel, signaler, maneuver, epaulet, harbor, reconnoiter, defense, pickax, Alfa, Whiskey, fire team.

British and American English (2) (p. 35)

British	American
leave	furlough
NAAFI	PX
petrol	gasoline
make ready	lock and load
int	intel
fire-trench	foxhole
bearing	azimuth
recce	recon
section	squad
depleted uranium	Staballoy

Slang (p. 36)

1. grunt 2. frag
3. liberate 4. take out
5. zap 6. aggro
7. civvy 8. chow
9. bull 10. rookie
11. boot camp 12. bandit

Armoured fighting vehicles (p. 37)

1. main battle tank 2. armoured car
3. infantry fighting vehicle
4. self-propelled anti-aircraft gun
5. self-propelled gun 6. light tank
7. armoured personnel carrier
8. multiple rocket launcher

Positions and locations (p. 38)

1. firing post 2. LZ
3. ammunition dump 4. POL point
5. bunker 6. command post
7. fire-trench 8. dressing station
9. vehicle check-point

Answer key

Categories 1: armoured fighting vehicles (p. 39)

MBT: Abrams, AMX-30, Challenger, Leopard, T-72
IFV: BMP, Bradley, Marder, Warrior
APC: AFV-432, BTR-80, M-113, MT-LB
SPG: Abbot, M-109, M-1974
CVR: BRDM, Scimitar

Categories (2): aircraft (p. 40)

Fighter: Eagle, Flanker, Flogger, Mirage, Phantom, Tomcat
Bomber: Backfire, Lancer, Spirit
Attack Helicopter: Apache, Cobra, Hind, Hip
Utility/Transport Helicopter: Blackhawk, Chinook, Hook, Huey, Puma

Categories (3): missiles (p. 41)

ATGW: Milan, Sagger, Spandrel, TOW
SAM: Blowpipe, Gaskin, Grail, Rapier, Sea Wolf, Stinger
AAM: AMRAAM, Aphid, Sidewinder, Sky Flash
Anti-ship: Exocet, Harpoon, Kormoran, Sea Eagle

PUZZLES AND QUIZZES

Word search (p. 44)

1. DETACHMENT
2. ROLL
3. TIN
4. ARMOUR
5. FORMATION
6. PARADE
7. RESERVE
8. IDENTITY
9. DETAIL
10. EXFILTRATE
11. ISSUE
12. DRUM
13. INSIGNIA
14. YIELD
15. CAMP
16. BRIGADE
17. SURVEILLANCE
18. TROOP
19. AIRLIFT
20. ORBAT
21. HEAT
22. EVADE
23. ELINT

Anagrams 1 (p. 45)

```
I N T E R C E|P|T
      F I G|H|T E R
          C|O|M P A N Y
          A|N|T H R A X
      F I R|E|F I G H T
        B A|T|T L E
          M|I|S S I O N
      E X E|C|U T I O N
      S Q U|A|D R O N
  C A M O U F|L|A G E
      S U P|P|O R T
          S|H|R A P N E L
    S I G N|A|L L E R
      B O M|B|A R D M E N T
      I N C|E|N D I A R Y
          S|T|I N G E R
```

Mystery term: PHONETIC ALPHABET

Military trivia 1 (p. 46)

1. lieutenant-general
2. Phantom
3. Soviet-designed 7.62mm assault weapon
4. decontamination
5. Czech-produced plastic explosive
6. the navy
7. as soon as possible
8. add the magnetic variation
9. 6,400
10. synthetic material used to make body armour, helmets, etc.
11. small pieces of fabric used as camouflage
12. division
13. the Red Crescent
14. the right-hand side of a ship or aircraft
15. 30mm Rarden cannon
16. mobile army surgical hospital
17. army chaplain
18. major general
19. Gurkha fighting-knife
20. one nautical mile per hour

Anagrams 2 (p. 49)

```
              |H|E L I C O P T E R
             D|E|M O L I T I O N
         A D V|A|N C E
     W I T H D|R|A W
         B A T|T|E R Y
           G A|S|O L I N E
       M E C H|A|N I Z E D
     O U T R A|N|G E
   C O M M A N|D|E R
         S U B|M|A R I N E
           B R|I|E F I N G
           C O|N|T R O L
             D|E|S T R O Y E R
           D I|S|T R E S S
```

Mystery Term: HEARTS AND MINDS

Military trivia 2 (p. 52)

1. time at which troops are woken up
2. cylindrical container mounted on a trailer
3. Lima
4. concrete pillars used as an obstacle for tanks
5. commander in chief
6. metal spikes designed to damage vehicle tyres
7. Huey
8. destroying enemy submarines
9. wardroom
10. American CH-53 heavy transport helicopter
11. the ground between the forward positions of two opposing forces
12. bomb which is simply dropped onto a target by an aircraft
13. anti-aircraft fire 14.safety catch
15. not allied to either side in a war
16. bridge supported by boats
17. forward line of own troops
18. improvised incendiary device consisting of a bottle of petrol with a wick
19. brigade major
20. the Pentagon

Military crossword (p. 53)

Across:
1. cookhouse
4. sonar
6. troop
7. transport
9. Alpha
11. RAP
12. coordinate
14. TEWT
16. range
19. victory
20. tank
21. notice
22. sensor
24. evasion
25. attack

Down:
1. contour
2. kennel
3. Scorpion
4. situation
5. replacements
8. PX
10. peace
13. advance
14. TAC
15. torpedo
17. antenna
18. gunboat
23. OK